**VICTORY**
*A World War II Bomber Pilot Memoir*
Douglas Coulter Richards

Published by Hellgate Press
(An imprint of L&R Publishing, LLC)
72 Dewey St.
Ashland, OR 97520
email: sales@hellgatepress.com

Book design: Michael Campbell
Cover design: L. Redding

ISBN: 978-1-954163-69-0

# VICTORY

## A WORLD WAR II BOMBER PILOT MEMOIR

✪ ✪ ✪

# DOUGLAS COULTER RICHARDS

15TH AIR FORCE
304TH WING
456TH BOMB GROUP H
746TH BOMB SQUADRON

# CONTENTS

# FOREWORD

I grew up with my grandfather Doug Richards telling tales of his time in World War II. On a few occasions, I traveled to some of the bomb group reunions he mentioned and got to explore some of the last surviving flyable B-24s with him as my tour guide. I am very grateful that he had the foresight to record his memories and thankful for the work his daughter, my mother, Beth Godfrey, put into getting his memoirs into book form in 1988. With the advent of geographic information system mapping, the research power of the internet, easy document editing, and so forth, I thought a new updated and improved version was due lest we forget the great aviators of yesteryear. For this version, I have created a number of new maps to help illustrate my grandfather's exploits, and many more pictures from his collection are also included, mixed into the narrative.

There is one tale that my grandfather told me that he did not include in this text, which is largely derived from my grandmother Mina Richards typing my grandfather's recollections in the early 1980s while he was looking through his documents. Many people have wondered what the B-24 aircrew did on long missions over hostile territory when it comes to using the bathroom. One time on a camping trip my grandfather, unprompted, told me they would take care of their business into glass jars and then chuck them out the window onto the enemy territory below.

I would also like to thank Gail Elliott Downs for her interview with Captain Wes Hyde regarding the Blechhammer mission. His additional perspective fleshes out the events and provides additional poignancy to what happened. Readers of this book will also likely enjoy her book *The Black Suitcase Mystery: A World War II Remembrance* which is about one of my grandfather's crew members, top turret gunner and radio operator George Rich. My grandfather, the rest of his crew, and the 456th Bomb Group as a whole are also all prominently featured. George Rich was her great-aunt's son, so her book has the same personal family connection as this book does for me.

— *David Godfrey*

# CHAPTER I:
# JOINING THE MILITARY

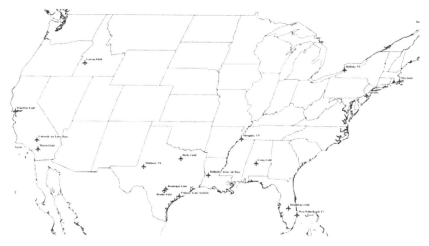

*Map of bases Douglas Richards visited.*
*Map by grandson David Godfrey.*

After graduating from high school in Lockport, New York, I worked on my father's farm a year before going to college. In 1936 through 1940 I was at Syracuse University in New York State, and while there was taking political science, which included international relations. At this time, there were many events that were happening in Europe with Hitler, and I realized at that particular time that war was inevitable and the United States would be drawn into it. We had an international relations professor who was also a colonel in the army, and by taking his course, I was able to verify this in a hurry. I graduated from Syracuse in 1940 with a bachelor's degree in business administration and started work in the fall in Buffalo, New York, making shock absorbers for Houdaille Manufacturing Company. We kept getting nearer to the conflict which had started between England, France, and Germany in 1939 when Germany invaded Poland. So, I knew it was just a matter of time.

I was classified 1-A, and in March of 1941, with the draft board breathing down my neck, I enlisted in the Army Air Force as a private. I was inducted and sworn in in Buffalo and took the train to Fort Dix, New Jersey, where I first experienced army life. There we learned how to drill and also do KP [kitchen police] and things like that. We were issued army clothes and after two, three, or four weeks, I don't know how long, we entrained for Selma, Alabama, where I was supposed to go into Research & Development (whatever that was!). I remember taking the train to Atlanta, and we had to change trains there, and I had my first Southern breakfast of grits, bacon, and eggs. This was a new experience for me.

*Leaving Fort Dix for Selma*

Selma, Alabama was a small, rural town about 60 miles from Maxwell Field, or I should say, Montgomery, Alabama. The Air Force base at Selma was brand new, so I was part of the work detail in getting that base ready. We had nice barracks to stay in; they were clean and so was everything else, and there I continued to learn about army life, but as far as the Research & Development, I never did see any part of that. I was soon in a work detail helping to clear a swamp area, which was between our barracks area and the flying field. They were going to make this into a lake. I soon found out, after I'd been there maybe two or three months, that this life was not for me, and since I had my college education I immediately started looking into the flying cadets as a way to change my work and my lifestyle. I was underweight, so I used to try to eat a lot, like bananas, and get my weight up. Finally, I was able to pass the physical. I believe it was around the first part of November that I was able to report to Hicks Field, Fort Worth, Texas.

Selma, Alabama was a typical southern country town, where people went to church on Sunday, and so we did that. It was a place where we could go into town and see the movies, and I believe that we were even invited out to dinner on a Sunday. We also used to hitchhike from Selma over to Montgomery and spend the weekend there. As I was only making $21.00 a month, and then got a raise to $30.00 a month, I didn't have a lot of money at the end of the month. But we still didn't have transportation or money for it. We would stay in a YMCA in Montgomery as we couldn't afford a hotel. I don't remember where we ate, but this wasn't any big problem. So, this was a chance to see a bigger city and relax a little bit.

*Warrens Corners, NY, Stone Road. Douglas Richards and his Irish Setter pheasant hunting. DCR was on his way from Selma, AL to Ft. Worth, TX for Flight School. Reported to Ft. Worth Nov. 15, 1941. It was great hunting.*

*Barracks at Selma*

*The author at the dynamite shed in Selma*

*Selma, AL, 1941. Barracks, Pvt Douglas C Richards (back row, left).*

*Selma, AL, 1941. Barracks, Pvt Douglas C Richards.*

*BT-13 Valiant*

Hicks Field was a small grass field outside of Fort Worth, Texas. It was run by civilians, and the instructors were civilians who were hired under contract, I suppose by the Air Force, to teach primary training to the cadets. This was a new lifestyle while at Hicks Field. We worked much harder, getting up early in the morning and working until late at night, taking much instruction. I see by the flight record that I flew 60 hours, and during that period of time I would have soloed. The record also tells about crashing the airplane on the first solo landing. We studied all kinds of things like aerodynamics, military rules and regulations, and just how to live as an officer in the Air Force. This was a good life; we ate well, we had good barracks, and it was an enjoyable period of time.

We used to spend our weekends at a good hotel in Fort Worth. We were there in Fort Worth on Sunday, December 7th, 1941, when Japan bombed Pearl Harbor. We hadn't necessarily expected this, but we did, of course, continue to expect to be drawn into the war in Europe. I don't remember anything particularly exciting or anything else at Hicks. Of course, the solo flight was the big thing, and then you were able to wear an identification bracelet around your wrist. This was an honor, and everyone looked forward to being able to wear that as your solo bracelet.

I was at Hicks Field from approximately November 15 to January 15 for two months of intensive training, and then I was assigned to Randolph Field in San Antonio, which was a very famous place at the time. I believe that it dated back to World War I, at least Brooks Field did. But Randolph was the showplace of the Air Force as far as training was concerned. It was modeled after the academies—West Point, etc. There were beautiful barracks and marching in formation.

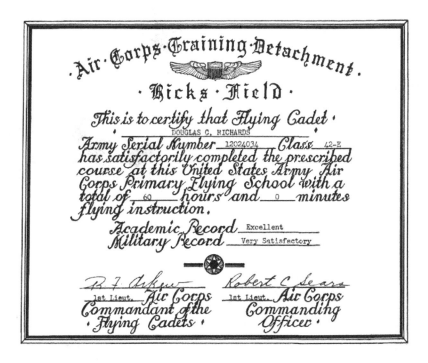

*Training certificate*

They had drill every day, and we would pass in review. Everything was very military. We were reprimanded and trained by the upperclassmen. They would make you stand in what we called a brace, which would be with our heads back and our chin in, our shoulders back, and just stand stiff. They'd make you stand that way for a considerable period of time. They called that "racking back" or something like that, but this was just part of the hazing that went on.

*Randolph Field, San Antonio, TX, 1942. Douglas C*
*Richards on parade ground with barracks in rear.*

We would march to the mess hall for our food. Early in the morning, say 6:00, we would be eating breakfast and we'd have to get out in formation. They would have a signal to tell us what kind of dress to wear. If it was raining, we'd wear a raincoat so all of the cadets would look alike every day, and we'd wear whatever the weather called for. We would march in formation into the big mess hall, and the underclassmen would have to sit on the edge of the chair, very erect, and very square. You'd pick up your knife and fork and you'd come up straight and then go straight into your mouth, and all that kind of stuff. Of course, your haircut was you might say almost bald—you were really clipped.

*Randolph Field, San Antonio, TX, 1942. Douglas C. Richards on parade ground with barracks in back, cannon for reveille.*

When talking about Randolph Field, we need to discuss the airplanes. The BT-13 was considerably larger than the PT-19. It was heavier and a lot more powerful. The biggest disadvantage of the BT-13 was that it would ground loop. When you landed the plane in a crosswind, if you didn't keep the airplane going down the runway correctly, the wind would catch it and swirl it around and would tip it up on one wheel and would drag a wing. Of course, this was a no-no in the service.

*Randolph Field, San Antonio, TX, March 14, 1942.*
*BT-13 airplane, Douglas C Richards.*

We graduated from Randolph March 15, 1942, and all I had to do was go across town to Brooks Field, which is on the south side of San Antonio. Brooks Field was an old WWI Air Force training base. It had the old barracks from WWI, and all the other facilities were of that date. It was still a good field with a lot of character. We had gravel runways but it was a good place to be. We enjoyed as cadets, San Antonio. It was strictly a military town with many retired military there, and Fort Sam Houston was a big infantry fort. That was in the center of the city. San Antonio had everything for the military. We got our taste of Mexican food, and we went to a rodeo, which was my first opportunity to witness one.

*Brooks Field, San Antonio, TX, 1942. Parade grounds.*

At Brooks we had our first retractable landing gear airplane, which would be an AT-6, which was the most famous and best-known trainer plane. It was a dandy airplane. It flew well and had great stability on landing and was enjoyable to fly. We could get up in the air when the cumulus clouds formed over Texas and play around in those clouds at 7,000 to 10,000 feet. It was enjoyable and likened to the hawks flying in the sky.

I contracted hepatitis while at Brooks Field. There were several of us in the hospital for a month, and that set me back in my graduation and obtaining my wings. That was the highlight of my career, obtaining my wings, and becoming a Second Lieutenant, an officer in the US Air Force.

*Brooks Field, San Antonio, TX, 1942. AT-6*
*(Advanced Training) airplane.*

*Brooks Field, San Antonio, TX, 1942. Picture taken*
*in an O-52 by one of the observers while we*
*were flying around. Douglas C Richards.*

*Brooks Field, San Antonio, TX, July 1942. Douglas C Richards.*

My folks came down to Texas, along with my aunt and Grandfather and Grandmother Coulter. My aunt was Elizabeth Smith. This was a big occasion for them, because they had never been to Texas before. They thoroughly enjoyed it. Dad drove an old Plymouth automobile down. We toured the city and had a great time.

# CHAPTER II:
## STATESIDE SERVICE

After graduating on July 3, 1942, at Brooks Field in Class 42E, I was assigned to fly observers around for about five weeks. We used what we called a pregnant duck. It was an O-52 airplane that had a big belly on it where the observer could get down and observe things. You had to crank the landing gear up, and as I remember, it took about 60 pushes and pulls of about a two foot stick to hydraulic lift the landing gear. This was the only plane I ever saw or flew that had such a retractable landing gear. This was an obsolete airplane and was no honor to fly. In fact, it was a terrible assignment. You did what they told you to do. It was nice to be able to stay in San Antonio a few more weeks as an officer and get a little more flying experience.

From there I was sent to DeRidder, Louisiana, from August 12 to October 30, 1942, as an observation pilot. This was not one of the best assignments either. In fact, being an observation pilot was not anything you would look up to. It was where they sent those pilots that probably were the poorest in the business. We flew little Cubs [Piper J-3] and Aeroncas [Aeronca L-3] around and dropped flour bags on some of the tank groups or infantry groups.

We tried to make war games at Camp Polk a little more realistic. I can remember those big war games, reading about them in the paper, and of course at that time, Camp Polk was one of the big army installations, probably dating back to WWI. DeRidder was a town where you would take the train from Lake Charles, Louisiana, straight north maybe 50 miles, right out in the middle of nowhere. The train had a cow-catcher out front and went about ten miles per hour. It had wooden passenger cars that had old lanterns hanging from the ceiling. It was really an obsolete moving stock.

*DeRidder, LA (maybe). Leaving for Palacios, TX October 31, 1942.*

On October 31, we transferred to Palacios, Texas, with the 5th Tow Target Squadron, another bum assignment. We stayed there until June 3, 1943, flying tow targets. I used to fly as much as I could to get the experience. To get a lot of night flying, we would fly for anti-aircraft searchlights. They would get those lights on you at about 6,000 to 8,000 feet and you could read a newspaper when they did.

*Palacios, TX, 1942. Douglas A-20 Havoc.*

*Palacios, TX, 1943. A-20, Douglas C Richards.*

At Palacios we learned how to fly a B-34. This is somewhat bigger than a DC-3. I believe it was made by Lockheed/Vega. It was a good airplane with big engines, and we really enjoyed it. It was fun getting checked out in something bigger than that little stuff that we had been flying.

At Palacios we had AT-11s. This was a Beechcraft modeled after Beechcraft's famous two-engine passenger plane. The AT-7 was the same plane used for navigator training, with the AT-11 used for bombardier training. We used to take the AT-11 and fly to Oklahoma City, New Orleans, etc., for the weekend. The staff car would take us into town, and we stayed at the best hotels. What a life!

At Palacios we went goose hunting. We would drive the Jeep and lift it over irrigation ditches and drive right through rice fields. We had goose dinner at Thanksgiving for the squadron. One time I flew the Cub to a town, Bayfield or somewhere [likely Bay City], and landed on one of the dirt roads and caught a ride into town to shop. This was a loosely run outfit. Saturday nights were spent at the Artillery Officers' Club.

This book has a picture of the results of our taking the Cub out to the island in the Gulf of Mexico and landing on the beach to fish. I broke my thumb turning the prop over to start it. The Commanding Officer (CO) said that trip was a NO-NO. We surf fished with mullet strips we caught on the beach. We could go out and get a plate of shrimp, a dozen for less than fifty cents.

*Palacios, TX, Camp Hular, 1942. Lt Fowler, Lt Douglas Richards. Fishing trip to Gulf of Mexico.*

*Palacios, TX. Lt Fowler and Lt Richards planned this fishing trip; flew a Piper Cub over to one of the Matagorda Islands and landed on beach.*

While at Palacios, I was given the opportunity to go up to Otis Field near Boston, Massachusetts, to ferry an O-47 from there back to Texas. I flew from Otis Field to Albany, New York, and followed the Erie Canal to Rochester, NY, and decided that I would buzz Barker, NY, a small town of 500 people. Barker is located on Lake Ontario and was the home of my aunt, Elizabeth Smith, one of my relatives who came to Texas for my graduation from pilot training school. This gave my aunt the opportunity to brag about me. I flew into Buffalo Municipal Airport, and my folks picked me up and took me home for a few days.

*Warrens Corners, NY, August, 1943. Richards farm, Douglas C Richards.*

Then I flew to Cincinnati, Ohio, and had my suitcase with all of my clothes stolen from me in the lobby of a big hotel. From Ohio I flew to Memphis, then to Little Rock, and eventually Palacios. I was weathered in in Memphis. The CO asked where I had been keeping myself when I finally returned to base.

Things were now opening up in Europe, where they needed pilots, so I was assigned to Hendricks Field, Florida, on July 16, 1943. We reported to Sebring, Florida, for B-17 training. After three weeks of intensive training, I learned how to fly a B-17. This was a tremendous experience. This plane was one of the easiest planes to fly. A tail dragger is always an easy plane to fly.

After training, I left on August 5th for home and leave. I had to report August 25, 1943, at Gowen Field, Boise, Idaho, to check out in the B-24 and at the same time pick up my crew.

### *List of Crew:*

Pilot, 1st Lieutenant Douglas Coulter Richards, Serial Number 0661129.

Copilot, 2nd Lieutenant Wilson Goodall, Serial Number 0811366.

Navigator, 2nd Lieutenant Robert B. Thompson, 0689692.

Bombardier, 2nd Lieutenant Daniel F. Curran 0688177.

Flight Engineer and Waist Gunner, Staff Sergeant Jerry Krenek, 38255748.

Radio Operator and Top Turret Gunner, Sergeant George E. Rich, 3111425.

Waist Gunner, Staff Sergeant Howard F. Shields, 12199048.

Ball Turret Gunner, Staff Sergeant Russell W. Brown, 35621109.

Tail Turret Gunner, Staff Sergeant John F. Litcher 3267625.

Nose Turret Gunner, Staff Sergeant Joseph G. Nickel 12168182.

*Crew No. 1 (left to right)*
*(in front) Sgt. Russell W. Brown, Bottom Turret Gunner;*
*(next row back) S/Sgt. Howard F. Shields, Top Turret Gunner;*
*(behind S/Sgt Shields) Lt. Daniel F. Curran, Bombardier;*
*Lt. Wilson Goodall, Copilot; Lt. Robert B. Thompson, Navigator;*
*Lt. Douglas C. Richards, Pilot;*
*(back row) S/Sgt John F. Litcher, Tail Turret Gunner,*
*S/Sgt Joseph G. Nickel, Nose Turret Gunner; Sgt George*
*E. Rich, Radio Operator and Waist Gunner; S/Sgt Jerry*
*Krenek, Flight Engineer and Waist Gunner*

# CHAPTER III:
# THE 456TH BOMB GROUP

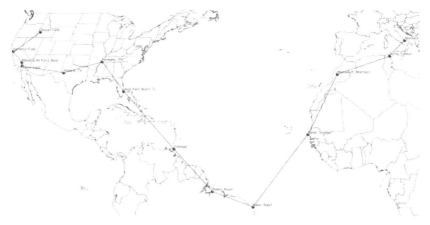

*Route taken to Europe by Douglas Richards.*
*Map by grandson David Godfrey.*

When the cadre of the 456th Bomb Group was formed in Boise, Idaho, Jocko Johnson was one of the lead bombardiers. They were up dropping practice bombs. Jocko decided to bomb the circular flower bed in front of the headquarters at the Mountain Home Air Force Base. He dropped a 100 lb. practice bomb on the flowers.

On September 16, 1943, we left for Edwards Air Force Base, Muroc Lake, California, for combat training. While there we learned as a crew, bombing, formation flying, and navigation. Whenever we had a weekend off, we would go to Los Angeles and Hollywood. We took in famous night clubs such as the Coconut Grove, Biltmore Bowl, and the Palladium. We took in famous radio shows and watched Bing Crosby make movies. That would be the one where he was a priest making the movie Going My Way. There was a lot of entertainment in Hollywood and Los Angeles. We got there perhaps once a month, about three or four times. We would ride in the back of a 6x6 Army truck. It was cold out in Muroc, so it wasn't a very pleasant ride.

*Muroc Lake. Brown, Mitchell, Rich, Shields (just been issued shoulder holster with 45-cal pistol, which they eventually took from us because it was impossible to fight our way out of Germany with it).*

*Muroc Lake, Edwards AFB, CA. Curran, Goodall.*

*Muroc Lake, Edwards AFB, CA. Richards,*
*Goodall—'Manifold Pressure Kid'.*

*Muroc Lake, Edwards AFB, CA, fall 1943. Douglas Richards,*
*Wilson Goodall, Robert Thompson, Daniel Curran.*

*Muroc Lake, Edwards AFB, CA, fall 1943. Nickel, Brown, Rich,*
*Curran, Krenek, getting equipment ready to go over.*

*Muroc Lake, Edwards AFB, CA, fall 1943. Rich, Nickel, just got Mae West life preservers issued to us.*

*Muroc Lake, Edwards AFB, CA, fall 1943. Thompson, Curran, with overseas equipment.*

*California, Muroc, Army Air Base. Changing B-24 engine at night.*

Early in December we left Muroc for Hamilton Field, San Francisco, to pick up a new B-24. We were on our way overseas. We were in San Francisco for just a few days, but we did get a chance to stay at the St. Francis Hotel in Chinatown.

The pipelines were full of airplanes on their way to Italy. We took a leisurely trip flying across country because of all the planes. We flew from San Francisco to March Field, Riverside, California, and from Riverside to Midland, Texas. I believe I went into town in Midland. From Midland we flew to Memphis, Tennessee. We stayed in Memphis several nights, and I remember going to the Peabody Hotel in the evening for refreshments. From Memphis we went to West Palm Beach, Florida. We waited until there was room in the pipeline for us to take off for Italy. Memphis and Midland were the only places where we got off base to go into town.

The night of December 23rd, 1943, we took off from West Palm Beach for Trinidad. I've always been sorry that we didn't fake some engine trouble and land in San Juan, Puerto Rico. On December 24th we flew from Trinidad to Belem, Brazil. The first time I saw a jungle close at hand was out the back door of the barracks. The density was awe-inspiring.

On Christmas Day we were flying down the coast of Brazil from Belem to Natal. We stayed at Natal a week or more. I checked the airplane out one day and proceeded to put it down on a deck over a beach. The swimmers took to the water for cover. We ate so much pineapple while at Natal that we got tired of it.

Everything was in order, and we took off for Dakar, Senegal, in Africa one night. Bob Thompson had a chance to use his sextant. We hoped its celestial navigation was accurate. It was a long trip. It must have been close to twelve hours. We played cards in the cockpit. The automatic pilot came in handy. We thought we could see Africa, and now I'm not sure we actually could. Finally, we got a signal on the radio compass. Dakar was cold, and I was surprised to see the tough Senegalese soldiers going around barefoot.

I was off the next day for Marrakech, Morocco. This is at high altitude, and I spent the coldest night of my life. We slept on Army cots with no mattresses. I don't think we had over one wool blanket. We were in these sheepskin-lined flying suits, but they didn't do much good. That cold air just permeated right up through that little canvas. We spent one night there.

From Marrakech we were on our way to Tunisia. The whole group was assembling there while our base in Italy was being made ready. The area was full of German tanks, etc. One of our pilots was killed by a landmine when we landed in Tunis.

Our crew went to a hotel in Tunis. It was a beautiful city with wide streets. We would go to American movies with Arabic captions. The Arabs would be in there smoking their Turkish tobacco. They reeked to high heaven.

One of the things I enjoyed most was visiting the Casbah. We were able to buy a kerosene lamp there that we needed. We were rationed one candle a week. One time we ended up scraping the wax off of our K rations and putting it in the lid of the can that the Spam came in. Then we put a string in the wax and that would be our candle so that we could play poker in the tent.

*Tunis, Tunisia. Entrance, Casbah, early 1944.*

One day I remember playing poker for twelve hours. I won $35 at nickel poker. That's quite a lot of money at those stakes. Then I started losing. We raised the ante to ten cents. I never wanted to lose money so I quit playing poker back in the squadron and started playing bridge.

While in Tunis, we enjoyed going into the city. Our crew was probably the only one who had transportation. Our engineer,

Krenek, had gone into a British junkyard and stole or smuggled whatever he needed of a vehicle and assembled it. I know he had to put a clutch in. He was a good auto mechanic, and he was able to fix up this old flatbed. It had no body but a couple of seats. The truck part was a little bigger than a half ton pickup truck. It had some wood in it. We could sit back there while Jerry Krenek would drive this truck back from Tunis to our base.

Our crew was probably the first one to have electricity in their tent. Krenek scrounged a big 12-volt generator run by gasoline. We had plenty of gasoline, because you could always drain it out of the airplanes if you had to. So, his tent had 12-volt electricity in it. We didn't have that, the officers' tent didn't, but he did.

While we were at the base flying field in Tunis, there was a fellow by the name of Sagar. He later went to Yale Divinity School. He tried to blow down a mess tent of a nearby group with his B-24. Well, he got caught at it. Colonel Steed or somebody (maybe our own Commanding Officer, Golden) made him write 500 times, "I will not strafe mess tents". But that was about all the reprimand there was to it.

*Tunis, base outside of Tunis, January 1944.*
*Goodall, Billings, Gordon Graham.*

I can remember our crew went out to test our airplane. We'd been there so long that we had to take our plane out just to practice and keep it running. We had a practice flight one day and tried to scare camels by buzzing them. We'd get that airplane down on the deck (low to the ground), and we'd fly lower than the windmills that were sitting there in the desert outside of Tunis.

Tunis was a French colony. It was very productive with their vineyards and wheat and grain. The Arabs did all the work.

I have somewhat pleasant memories of Tunis. It was a beautiful city. In Tunis we had our stove, and also in Italy. The government never gave you anything. You had to scrounge it or steal it to supply your own needs. It wasn't in their orders.

We would make a stove out of a metal ammunition can that ammunition was shipped in. It would be about two and a half feet long, eight to ten inches high and eighteen inches wide. We would cut a hole in the front of it and run a copper tube in there from a 55-gallon drum. It had a shut-off valve. We would run the tubing into the stove. To make the chimney for the stove, you'd cut a hole in the top and bend it up. We'd take an 88- or 90-millimeter shell, which is tapered on one end, and cut the other end off. Because it was tapered on the end where it held the bullet, we could stack one of these shells on top of another and use this for our chimney through the top of the tent. We would turn the gas on. This would be 100 octane fuel out of the airplane or whatever we could get. We'd light that and burn it.

Sometimes if that stove was hot and a guy didn't know about it, we'd turn the gas on a little ahead of time, and we'd the tell the fellow to light it and of course it would explode with a loud and vicious explosion. It would lift the thing right off the floor. No one ever got hurt. Sometimes we'd turn the gas on and load the thing up with fumes and run toilet paper from the stove out the tent door and light the toilet paper and watch the thing explode. That shows how dumb we were and how we had to entertain ourselves with these stupid things we did.

# CHAPTER IV:
## COMBAT

*Map of bombing targets. Map by grandson David Godfrey.*

Eventually, after we were at Tunis a long while, our bomb group went up to Cerignola, Foggia, Italy. We flew up there and set up housekeeping under the olive trees. We were one of hundreds of bombers in the Foggia area.

*Italy, mess hall, 746th*

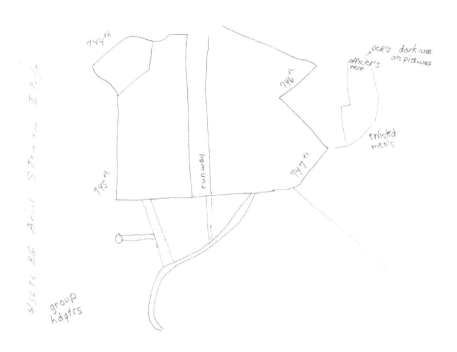

*Cerignola, Italy, 456th Bomb Group Air Base*

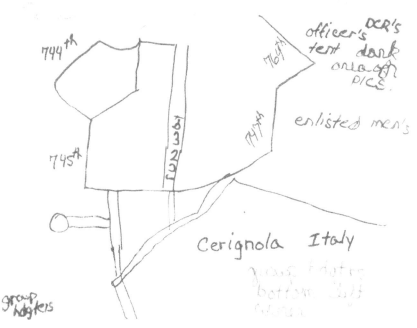

*Cerignola, Italy, 456th Bomb Group Air Base*

As I look over the missions I flew, it is hard to talk about all of them, but I will briefly describe or try to remember whatever might be pertinent as far as I'm concerned.

(front row, left to right)
T/Sgt Bomber Crew Chief; Sgt Russell Brown, Ball Turret Gunner;
S/Sgt Joseph Nickel, Nose Turret Gunner; S/Sgt Howard Shields, Waist
Gunner; S/Sgt John Litcher, Tail Turret Gunner; Sgt George Rich, Radio
Operator and Top Turret Gunner; S/Sgt Jerry Krenek, Waist Gunner
and Engineer; Cpl Bonomo, Ground Assistant Crew Chief.

(back row, left to right)
Lt Wilson Goodall, Copilot; Lt Daniel Curran, Bombardier; Lt
Bob Thompson, Navigator; Lt Douglas Richards, Pilot.

Front row l-r
S/sgt. Jerry Krenek -waist gunner, engineer
Sgt. Russell Brown - Ball Turrett gunner
S/sgt. John Litcher- Tail Turret gunner
S/sgt. Howard Shields -waist gunner
S/sgt. Joseph Nichel - nose turret gunner
Sgt. George Rich - radio operator, top turret gunner  kia

back row (officers) l-r
Lt. Daniel Curran- Bombadier
Lt. Wilson Goodall- Copilot  kia
Lt. Robert Thompson- navigator kia
Lt. Douglas Richards - pilot

Crew in Italy 1944

The first mission, February 10, 1944, was to a little town in northern Italy. It wasn't very far from Cassino, and it didn't really amount to anything. It lasted only 3 hours and 45 minutes. It was sort of a milk run and a chance to get the crew tested out under combat conditions.

*Bombing, 1944. B-24 on way over Adriatic.*

*Bombing, 1944–45. Flak over target.*

*Bombing, 1944–45. Squadron plane*
*dropping bombs through overcast.*

The first one of any great importance was on March 15, 1944, to Monte Cassino. This was somewhat famous, because some of the Air Force bombed our own troops. As a result of that, the ground forces weren't too friendly towards us. We were probably quite ineffective. Cassino was a major obstacle to our ground forces in their drive towards Rome. I've read about this many times since then. It took a great deal of fighting by many troops, mainly the British, to conquer Monte Cassino. I have pictures further back in my war photo album showing Monte Cassino when we were going to Rome one day by jeep. It certainly was devastated, but this wasn't from our bombing necessarily, but from our own artillery, etc.

*Abbey of Mount Cassino, Italy, 1944. Picture taken shortly after abbey taken by our troops on road to Rome. Capt Collins, Sq Adjutant; Capt. Olmstead, Sq Engineer; and Capt. Snee.*

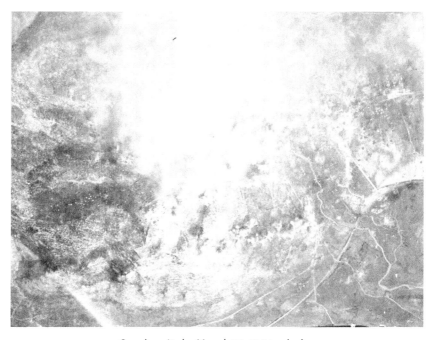

*Cassino, Italy, March 15, 1944 mission*

I can remember bombing at Rimini. We later called it a milk run. Rimini is on the coast of the Adriatic. We could come in off the Adriatic and make our bomb run and get back out to the safety of the Adriatic. I don't remember any enemy fighters on these trips in northern Italy.

*Rimini, Italy, March 24, 1944. Mission: marshalling yard.*

I remember bombing Maniago in northern Italy about March 26th, 1944. Maniago was a grass airfield above Venice in the plateau at the head of the Adriatic. We used a fire or magnesium bomb at that time, which would explode above the ground and send magnesium onto the ground.

*Cerignola, Italy, 1944. Purple Shaft crew.*

*Verona, Italy, March 28, 1944. Mission: marshalling yard.*

*Milan, Italy, March 29, 1944. Mission: marshalling yard.*

Palm Sunday 1944 was held in the big Group building, which was used to store wine vats when the Italians had it. I went to that service. We didn't go to church very often. Dan Curran went regularly to Mass, and some of us went occasionally to church.

*Cerignola, Italy, Palm Sunday 1944. Group Headquarters,*
*Douglas Richards attended this service.*

*Cerignola, Italy, Palm Sunday service 1944. Group Headquarters.*

The next mission of any importance to me, at least at this point, was Bad Voslau, Austria, on April 12, 1944. This was an aircraft factory situated just outside of Vienna. We encountered very strong enemy fighters on the way up over Yugoslavia. As a result of this, our best friends, as far as crews were concerned, were shot down. It was the Townsend crew that went down that day. They were flying right under me leading an element of three airplanes. We were under continuous fighter attack on the way in towards Vienna. They were shot down there, and I've never heard that any of them got out alive. It seems as though they would have, but the crew never reported parachutes and I've never heard that they came out alive. On that same mission we had a hit by, I always said, a rocket. There were 400 to 500 holes put in our airplane. The back end of it was like a sieve. As result of that hit, Krenek, our waist turret gunner and aircraft mechanic, was wounded. Krenek wasn't seriously hurt, but he did of course get the Purple Heart from it. He continued to fly.

*Bad Vöslau (near Vienna), April 12, 1944. Bombing aircraft factory, 11th sortie of Douglas Richards.*

*Cerignola, Italy, April 12, 1944. Purple Shaft damaged over Munich, direct hit, Bad Vöslau, Austria, aircraft factory.*

*Cerignola, Italy, 1944. Lt Richards (rt) receiving 1st DFC. Col Steed, Group Commander, after Bad Vöslau, Austria, mission.*

RESTRICTED

HEADQUARTERS
FIFTEENTH AIR FORCE
APO     520

C-BGW-bmr

GENERAL ORDERS )
:
NUMBER    242 )

4 June 1944.

SECTION V -- AWARDS OF THE DISTINGUISHED FLYING CROSS AND/OR OAK LEAF CLUSTER
FOR THE DISTINGUISHED FLYING CROSS

Under the provisions of AR 600-45, as amended, and pursuant to authority
contained in Circular No. 26, Headquarters MATOUSA, 6 March 1944, the Distinguished
Flying Cross and/or Oak Leaf Cluster for the Distinguished Flying Cross, in the
categories as listed, is awarded the following named officers, residence as
indicated, with the following citation:

For extraordinary achievement in aerial flights as lead personnel of a
heavy bombardment group, on a vitally important bombing mission against a heavily
defended enemy aircraft factory in Austria on 23 April 1944. Despite heavy enemy
opposition of both intense and accurate fighter and antiaircraft fire, displaying
outstanding coolness, leadership and cooperation in holding their formation
closed up for maximum fire power against the enemy, these men brought their group
over the target for a highly successful bombing run. The objective was completely
destroyed, nullifying the output of enemy aircraft from this large factory.
Turning from the target, they again brought their formation through the enemy
defenses for a safe return to base without loss. By their outstanding professional
skill, courage and devotion to duty, together with their exceptional teamwork
under such hazardous conditions, these men have reflected great credit upon
themselves and the Armed Forces of the United States of America.

DISTINGUISHED FLYING CROSS

FREDERICK W. HYDE, O-24923, Captain, Air Corps, 746th Bombardment Squadron,
456th Bombardment Group, United States Army. Residence at appointment:
Knoxville, Tennessee.

DOUGLAS C. RICHARDS, O-661129, First Lieutenant, Air Corps, 746th Bombardment
Squadron, 456th Bombardment Group, United States Army. Residence at appointment:
Lockport, New York.

DANIEL P. CURRAN, O-683177, Second Lieutenant, Air Corps, 746th Bombardment
Squadron, 456th Bombardment Group, United States Army. Residence at appointment:
St. Louis, Missouri.

By command of Major General TWINING:

R. K. TAYLOR,
Colonel, GSC,
Chief of Staff.

OFFICIAL:

/s/ J. M. Ivins,
J. M. IVINS,
Lieutenant Colonel, AGD,
Adjutant General.

A TRUE EXTRACT COPY:

JOHN M. COLLINS, CAPT, AC.

*Turnu Severin Air Drome April 16, 1944.*
*12th sortie of Douglas Richards.*

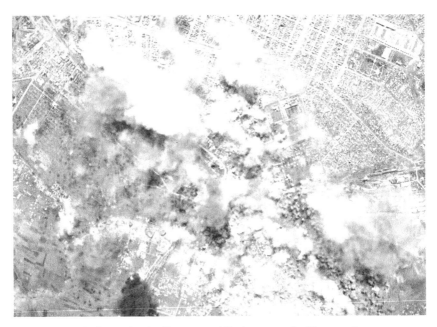

*Sofia, Italy, April 17, 1944. Mission: marshalling yard.*

*Milan, Italy, April 30, 1944. Bombing marshalling yard, railroad engine turntable at upper left. 16th sortie of Douglas Richards, TSgt Ash KIA.*

It wasn't very long after the Bad Voslau bombing that we went over in the Ploesti area in Romania. The records show that I went into Bucharest. Ploesti is a suburb, so to speak, of Bucharest. It isn't very far from it. We were presented with the same problems that happened every time we went into Ploesti, and that was terrific anti-aircraft fire. We used to say we could get out and walk on it. It would explode and it would shake the airplane and the shrapnel would rattle around in the bomb bay and in the back end of the airplane, or wherever. It seemed that every mission we went on we got hit by either enemy aircraft or with flak.

*Bucharest, Hungary, May 7, 1944. Bombing marshalling yard.*
*18th sortie of Douglas Richards, Peterson in bottom right corner.*

*Italy, Maj Douglas C Richards*

*Italy, Gin Ray: 170 missions, 891 combat hours. SSgt Raymond
J Glassner, Crew Chief, 746th, Perleberg, Germany.*

Bucharest missions and two or three Ploesti missions were
quite serious. They were surely not milk runs. I can remember

on a Ploesti run one day, looking back and being able to see the smoke from the fires in the oil refineries rising as high as we were, 20,000 to 22,000 feet.

We always encountered enemy fighters, like the Focke-Wulf 190. I could see them come in so close that you could see the pilot in the cockpit. They caused us almost as much trouble as the terrible flak.

One of our crew friends right back of us and just below us was blown out of the sky over Ploesti one day. He was one of those real nice young fellows that graduated from West Point, Assistant Operations Officer, by the name of Beck. It was something we didn't look forward to. Missions were assigned with no thought to the severity of them. You took your turn. We enjoyed the milk runs, but we didn't have very many of them. It was like the roll of the dice.

note smoke generators along R.R. track

*Ploesti, Romania, May 5, 1944. Bombing oil refinery.*

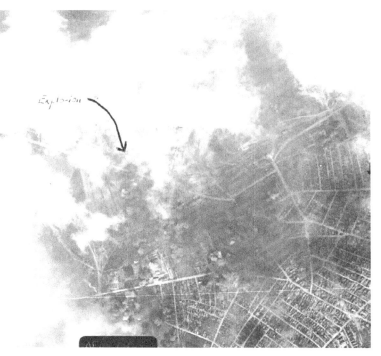

*Ploesti, Romania, May 5, 1944. Bombing refinery.*

*Ploesti, Romania, May 18, 1944. Explosion of fuel at oil field refinery. 20th sortie of Douglas Richards.*

Munich is listed here for June 9 and another for June 13. I don't remember which was which. We were bombing aircraft factories next to an airport. We received a direct hit in the airplane after we dropped the bombs over the target. It blew a gaping hole maybe three to four feet in diameter in the back end of the airplane, right behind the ball turret gunner. He was shook up but not injured and was able to get out of the ball turret. The only real damage was that we lost our trim tab, so consequently we had to exert pressure on the stick or wheel to keep our nose down. It did shake us up a bit. That hit didn't explode or we wouldn't be here today. It went right through the top of the airplane. The enemy 88mm anti-aircraft shells had altitude fuses on them, and they weren't set at our altitude, so instead it made a gaping hole.

*Munich, Germany, May 24, 1944. Direct hit by German 88mm gun. Krenek's heel shattered. 21st sortie of Douglas Richards.*

LUCKY ESCAPE—1st Lieut. Douglas C. Richards, (right) 26, son of Mr. and Mrs. William H. Richards, RFD 1, pilot of the B-24 Liberator bomber, the "Purple Shaft," smiles "it's lucky this hole wasn't someplace else or we wouldn't be here to tell about it," as he examines the damage done by German flak during a bombing mission over Germany. His co-pilot, Lieut. Daniel F. Curran Jr., of St. Louis, Mo., also breathes a relief. Lieut. Richards was awar' ' '' DFC for a subsequent raid on enemy airfields in Austria.

FLAK DOWNS AMERICAN PLANE OVER GERMANY

BLAZING LIBERATOR bomber careens over, spills bombs after being hit by flak during attack on Blechhammer, Germany; crew members are unaccounted for. Both bombers are from Italy-based U. S. 15th Air Force, which has been raiding southern German, Austrian and Czechoslovak targets. To halt American assaults, Germans have sent some new jet-propelled fighters to Italian front.

The Public Relations Department at Group sent pictures and stories to the home front to cheer the people up. I'm not sure how much cheering it did, but they used to send these press releases to our homes, for the public. When we got back to the base, the tower called us and told us they could see this gaping metal hanging down. But that wasn't so [the ball turret wasn't down], so we came on in and landed.

Krenek's heel was crushed like it was in a vise from this direct hit. He was never able to walk correctly after that. He came from Texas and was a good engineer. That was the end of his combat. He went home after this mission.

Our airplane, the Purple Shaft, was retired after the Munich mission. We had had that plane since Hamilton Field, San Francisco. Goody named it the Purple Shaft because he figured he was getting shafted by flying in a bomber. He wanted to fly in a fighter. The Purple Shaft was green; later B-24Js were silver.

SECRET

ORGANIZATION 746TH BOMBARDMENT SQUADRON (H)

PAGE   ＃3         WAR DIARY       STATION: STORNARA FIELD
MONTH OF JUNE                       LOCATION: STORNARA, ITALY
PREPARED BY C. E. MARR        RANK & BRANCH CPL, AIR CORPS

DAY                                  EVENTS
THIRTEENTH: "The Purple Shaft" seems to have been ill fated from it's
beginning. Again, as on the 23rd of May, it received a direct hit in
the waist. Also, as before, S Sgt Jerry Krenek was injured. Injured
with him this time was T Sgt George E. Rich, Radio Operator.

Over the target, Munich, S Sgt Brown from his position, ball
turret, (A/C 489) could see the flak bursting excitedly ahead.
"Flak-wise" from many similiar missions he soon realized that their
ship was being tracked. Directly, forward, a burst, and then again.
Realizing that a third burst would be near his position in the ball,
he unlatched and threw open the hatch door. Whami The flak hit.
The force of the blast exploding just forward of his position, threw
him out of his turret and up through the open hatch. A bump on the
head and couple of pieces of flak are his only momentos of this "near-
miss".

The boys in the waist did not escape as easily. The flak when
it burst, tore away the flooring in the waist. The ship rocking from
the blast and feeling the floor give way beneath him, Krenek, (L/G)
clutched his safety strap and gun. Rich from the opposite waist
position, saw Krenek slipping through thewrent flooring. He threw
off his oxygen mask and grabbed for him. Seizing him by his
parachute harness, he pulled him to safety. It was then he noticed
that Krenek was seriously wounded. Flak fragments had torn into his
feet and legs. Rich immediately began first aid. Breathing with
difficultly, he attempted to put his oxygen mask back on. There was
no oxygen. The system had been smashed by the same blast that had
torn a hole through the ship and had wounded Krenek. There was a
portable oxygen bottle intact. This, he gave to Krenek, sacrificing
his comfort to the greater needs of the wounded man.

Litcher, from his place in the tail, started forward to see if
he could help. Rich motioned him back. As Litcher said later, "I
thought as long as Krenek was being taken care of, that I had better
get back to those tail guns. We would be 'Dead Pigeons' with no
waist guns nor ball turret if I were out of the tail." He said later,
" When I climbed back into my turret, I had my flak suit off and my
chute on. You know, the tail was so woobly, that every little jolt
felt as though the tail was going to crack off the ship."

Off oxygen and at lower altitude, Rich who had been too busy with
Krenek to notice, realized that he himself had been wounded. Lt.
Curran, bombardier, came back to the waist and administered first aid
to Rich.

This was the shafts last combat mission. Back at the field,
Krenek was rushed to Foggia hospital for emergency treatments and
Rich with lesser wounds to Cerignola.

**SECRET**

When you had wounded aboard, you'd shoot off what we called
a Very pistol, which shot a red flare that would alert the ambulance that was sitting at the end of the runway. So, we'd just pull
up at the end of the runway, and the ambulance would take the
wounded away.

One time we came back with a very seriously wounded camera-man aboard. He may have died from his wounds, I don't know. I don't know his name. Dan Curran, our bombardier, was our doctor aboard ship. He would go back and give the fellow a shot of morphine, which we carried aboard as part of our medical kit. But this fellow was very seriously injured, and so we landed at the end of the runway.

Louis Trippi (our flight surgeon) and our CO, and the ambulance were standing there. They were in the process of getting the wounded out of the bomb bay area, and another airplane was coming in. It looked as though it was going to crash right into us. It was very low. I don't remember now what was the trouble with that airplane, but we thought it was going to crash. We were all standing around, and I hollered at the ambulance, "Get it out of here!" Well, the driver backed up. Goodall, my copilot, happened to be standing in back of the ambulance, and the ambulance backed over him. Well, Goody before that was pretty well shaken up anyway and wanted to go home. So I'm sure that he was thinking as a result of this he could go home. He was taken up to the group dispensary. When I got up there, I thought he was half drunk from drinking some of the whiskey. I don't know how he ever got a hold of it. He went into the Foggia hospital about 20 miles from our place. I went up to see him. There wasn't anything wrong with him. He was a little bit disappointed about that whole situation, because he was ready to go home. He lost his life on the Blechhammer raid that I'll mention later.

*Italy, Ferrara Air Drome June 10, 1944. 23rd sortie of Douglas Richards, Frederick J. Steele, photographer, 746th, KIA August 22, 1944.*

*Hungary, Karlova Air Drome June 28, 1944. 25th sortie of Douglas Richards, Donald L Sloss, photographer, 747th.*

*Hungary, Karlova Air Drome June 28, 1944. 25th sortie of Douglas Richards, Theodore Kogut, photographer, 747th.*

*Hungary, Karlova Air Drome June 28, 1944.*
*25th sortie of Douglas Richards.*

*Munich, Germany, 1944. Marshalling yard, bomb off target.*

**April 15.** Target--Budapest M/Y, Hungary. We were unable to bomb
this primary target. Secondary Target--Nis M/Y, Yugoslavia.
Result: Excellent.

**April 16.** Target--Brasov, Roumania. We bombed the Turma-Severin
A/D and Dispersing Area. Result: Excellent.

**April 17.** Target--Sofia M/Y, Bulgaria. No fighters; little flak.
Result: Excellent.

**April 20.** Target--Trieste, Italy. There was a heavy undercast
which obscured the target; thus, the bombs were dropped in a field.
All planes returned safely.

**April 21.** Target--Bucharest M/Y, Roumania. This was a rather bad
day , from the standpoint that were the recall transmitted by the
Fifteenth Air Force heard by our operators, much damage would have
been averted. As it was, heavy flak and inclement weather had to
be contended with. Lt. Tavel's crew had to land at the 318th and
319th Fighter Group landing field with only two engines operating
and a dangerously low gas supply. Four men: S/Sgt Pomering, Guthrie,
Billingsly, and Horton bailed out prior to the plane's landing.
Result: Poor.

**April 23.** Target--Bad Voslau, Austria. On this mission we ran into
from 100 to 150 ME 109's and FW 190's and extremely heavy flak over
the target. When fifteen enemy planes pounced on Lt. Townsend and
his crew, the damage done was irreparable. Nine parachutes were seen
to open as the plane spun to the ground. S/Sgt Ramsey, flying on his
first mission and a new replacement on Lt. Richards' crew, was

-4-

**SECRET**

seriously injured by a rocket entering the plane and bursting near him. Captain Tripi, our doctor, flew him to the Bari General Hospital. Lt. Goodal, co-pilot on the same Lt. Richards' crew, was also injured on our own runway. While getting the injured man from the planes, a plane from the 745th Squadron appeared to be trying for a crash landing. Everybody scrambled for safety; Sgt. Cameron hopped into the ambulance in an attempt to drive it to safety. In the swirl of dust, he did not see our co-pilot and backed over his upper thigh. Lt. Goodal was removed to the Foggia Hospital.

April 24. Target--Bucharest, Roumania. Six ships of our squadron took off, but three returned early. No fighters were encountered and very little flak. The M/Y were left in shambles. S/Sgt Ramsey died of the wounds he received the previous day.

April 25. Target--Turin, Italy. Lt. Lehner returned early. Lt. Robert S. Ensign's crew struck flak south of Florence and momentarily lost control; he directed the crew to "hit the silk". Lt. Abrams, bombardier, and Sgt. Mordick, nose gunner, did so. In the meanwhile, Lt. Ensign regained control and brought the ship home with the hydraulic system leaking badly. All other ships returned safely. Result of the mission: Successful.

April 28. Target--Porto San Stefano. Result--Unsatisfactory.

April 30. Target--Milan Lambrate M/Y. Result--Successful.

-5-

**SECRET**

VII. CASUALTIES.

| NAME | TYPE |
|---|---|
| 2nd Lt. Goodal, Wilson NMI | Injured on runway |
| 2nd Lt. Thomson, Robert Q. | Flak wounds |
| T/Sgt Krenek, Jerry NMI | Flak wounds |
| S/Sgt Monroe, John P. | 25 exploded shell holes in body, face, legs, and hands |
| S/Sgt Ramsey, Harlow R. | Wounded in action and died as a result |
| S/Sgt Schroeder, Robert E. | Flak wounds |

VIII. MISSING IN ACTION

Capt. Townsend, John C.
2nd Lt. Abrahams, Robert NMI
2nd Lt. Graham, Gordon L.
2nd Lt. Linberg, Herbert E.
2nd Lt. Webb, Edwin J.
T/Sgt Kensinger, Leslie C.
S/Sgt Bashaw, Leon P.
S/Sgt Crowe, Arthur L.
S/Sgt Duncan, Glenn E.
S/Sgt Feuerstein, Louis W.
S/Sgt Marston, Douglas C.
S/Sgt Mordick, Lavern F.

-6-

Another mission that stands out was Friedrichshafen in Germany on July 20, 1944. It is on Lake Constance, across from Switzerland. The lighter-than-air aircraft, such as the Graf Zeppelin and the Hindenburg, were all made here. We didn't bomb it because of that kind of aircraft though, I believe there was an aircraft factory there. That was one of the places where, if you were going to be hit, we sort of wanted to be hit, because we could just glide across the lake, and ditch it or bail out over Switzerland. That would have been any easy way to spend the rest of the war. We didn't get hit and flew on home.

One of the planes of the 456th Bomb Group was flying a mission near the Switzerland border after coming away from the target. The pilot said over the intercom to the crew, "If you hear me say 'Bail out!', do it." One of the crewmen in the waist of the plane heard him say, "Bail out!" and so he bailed out. He landed in Switzerland. They shipped him home to the USA because they didn't appreciate him jumping out.

After Friedrichshafen, on August 13, 1944, we bombed the railroad bridge in Orange, in southern France. I remember there were several groups. We were the last squadron, and we were flying one squadron behind another on the railroad bridge, which was precision bombing. The bridge hadn't been hit. When we flew in there, the flak was just so terrible that I thought I would never get through, and I'm sure the rest of the crew felt the same way. The sky was blackened with the shells exploding around us. They knocked out one of our engines, and we were hit in many places. Curran, our bombardier, was able to bomb that bridge, and I have pictures in the book somewhere to show that bridge being hit.

This was one of those missions you never forget. This was at the time of the invasion of southern France, when our ground troops were going in there, and we wanted to cut off any possible chance of the Germans reinforcing what troops they did have in southern France. That was the reason that we went in there. We flew back over Sardinia I believe. We were banged up a little bit, but we were used to having one engine out when we came back, so this was standard operational procedure.

*Orange, France, August 13, 1944. Targeting railroad bridge. Douglas Richards' was the last squadron and bridge had not been hit yet. His bomb hit it.*

*Orange, France, August 13, 1944. Targeting
railroad bridge to support the southern France
invasion. 29th sortie of Douglas Richards.*

*Orange, France, August 13, 1944. Targeting
railroad bridge to support the southern France
invasion. 29th sortie of Douglas Richards.*

*Sortie 31 of Douglas Richards, Italy,*
*Avisio Viaduct August 28, 1944.*

*Sortie 32 (1) of Douglas Richards, Yugoslavia,*
*Szeged railroad bridge September 3, 1944*

*Sortie 32 (2) of Douglas Richards, Yugoslavia,*
*Szeged railroad bridge September 3, 1944*

*Sortie 33 of Douglas Richards, Italy, San Dona*
*Di Piave railroad bridge October 10, 1944*

*Italy, Sgt Louis J Foehrenbacher (hand in piston that blew up on mission),
Koch, maybe Siegfried Koch, (on left), Anthony P Haggis, all 746th*

*Italy, Sgt Louis J Foehrenbacher (on left), SSgt Silvio A
Bellofatto, Whitestone, Long Island, New York, both 746th*

*Italy, winter of 1944. Sgt Louis J*
*Foehrenbacher, engine cost $9000.*

*Italy, Stornara 1944. Sgt Louis J Foehrenbacher (on*
*left), MSgt Lawrence Tolosano, both 746th.*

*Marshalling yard*

# CHAPTER V:
# THE BLECHHAMMER MISSION

The Blechhammer run was on August 22, 1944. It was one I will never forget. I made two runs there, according to the records, but I don't remember going there the second time. We sweated out going there for some time. We knew it was going to be one of the roughest missions we would ever go on. I notice that the round trip-time for the first mission was 8 hours and 15 minutes. The October 13 mission only lasted 5 hours and 50 minutes. We must not have gone all the way to Blechhammer, but aborted. We didn't go all the way back to Italy after flying to Blechhammer on the August mission, just to Vis off the coast of Yugoslavia.

Blechhammer was a synthetic oil refinery situated in southwest Poland, 75 miles west of Krakow, in a region called Lower Silesia, in what used to be a part of eastern Germany. A modern atlas won't show any place named Blechhammer, but there is a town named Ujazd very near that place inside the current boundaries of Poland. There are two places called Ujazd in Poland, but this is the one near Kedzierzyn and Slawiecice near Opole. I remember hearing about Poland in the news. Silesia is where coal mines and fields are in Poland. We were hitting this synthetic oil refinery. This was an important target for us. The strategy of the Air Force was to knock out the oil. When refineries were knocked out, the oil that airplanes and motor transports used was stopped, the vehicles wouldn't be able to run, and we would have a free hand. This we accomplished at this time. Ploesti was no longer a factor. The only things left were this synthetic oil refinery and the one at Odertal, only a few miles southwest of Blechhammer. Odertal was hit by another wing at the same time we struck our target at Blechhammer. This was an important mission, and we knew it would be a dangerous mission. This was the first time we went there.

I was flying as the command pilot with Captain Hall as the first pilot. As I said previously, the first pilot does most of the flying of the airplane; the command pilot is in charge of the lead aircraft and makes decisions about the mission for the squadron or group. There are seven planes in a squadron and four squadrons in a group. We were flying squadron lead. The plane on my right, which was deputy lead, was flown by my copilot, Goodall, from Scranton. The deputy lead flies on the command pilot's wing, and the deputy command in that plane takes over the duties of the command pilot in case the lead plane has to abort its mission or is shot down. Goodall actually had my crew in his airplane. He was flying as the first pilot. With him was Captain Hyde, Operations Officer at the time, and I was Assistant Operations Officer. He was flying as Goody's copilot or deputy command pilot.

On the day before going to Blechhammer, my crew had flown with the group to strike an airfield in far eastern Hungary; it was the 49th (or next to last) mission for Goody and the other members of our original crew. Hyde flew that mission too, but with another crew. The group only lost one airplane on that one. Hyde was scheduled to take a five-day leave to Rome on the next day, the 22nd. However, Goody went to see him after the August 21st mission to tell him that the crew had requested that he ask Hyde to take them on their 50th and last mission. Hyde asked him when they wanted to go, and Goody said they would leave that to him. Hyde said "Okay, we'll go tomorrow."

Heavy bombardment wings had four groups. When the B-24 wings attacked a target, the lead group always flew at an altitude of 20,500 feet and the next two groups always flew at 21,500 and 22,500 feet. The fourth group flew at 19,500 feet. Our group always flew in the third position except when assigned to the lead position. Jerry (the Germans) was not stupid, so he always cut the fuses to make the shells explode at those fixed altitudes for each group. However, after our group demonstrated its ability to fly really tight formations at 25,000 feet, it was authorized to fly at 24,500 feet when flying in its normal third position. On August 22nd, 1944, our group flew the bomb run at 24,500 feet. There was no flak at our level on the bomb run that day. There was no flak until we cleared the target, nor were there any fighters in the vicinity at any time.

*Sortie 30 of Douglas Richards. Blechhammer, Germany, August 22, 1944. Bombing synthetic oil refinery, 746th lost 3 planes, and 11 men KIA.*

At the briefing that morning we were told that other targets in the area were being hit at the same time. To avoid flying over those targets and their flak batteries, the group leader was instructed to turn left only 5 to 10 degrees from the north-westerly heading of the bomb run and to hold that heading for 15 to 20 minutes before starting a very slow turn south to the heading for home.

After their (Goody's) bombs went away, Hyde took over the controls to give Goody a rest and then expressed his relief and optimism on the intercom. Litcher replied from the tail, "Let's not count our chickens too soon," or words to that effect. Then suddenly the group leader (Ladd, the Group Operations officer and leader of the Blechhammer mission) put us into a steep, diving turn south and dropped us to about 17,500 feet right over the adjacent target of Odertal. The group leader leveled out there and Jerry's flak batteries took over. The first stick of about six or eight shells came tracking up from the rear and the right of Goody's aircraft and blew off the tip of his right wing. Hyde moved in toward our aircraft as tightly as possible, which may have been a mistake. The next stick of six or eight shells came up again from the rear, and one exploded in the root of the left wing. The left wing fell away and the aircraft burst into flames. After turning in a tight spin for a few turns, it exploded. What was important here was the tremendous size of these shell bursts and the accuracy of the guns. None of us had seen them before, and our intelligence officers had never told us about them. These shells were larger than the 88mm; they were 150mm.

As soon as Goodall heard the explosion, he left his seat without his chute. Goodall had a premonition that his plane would be blown up. Goodall was scared stiff. Hyde wrote his fiancée that he would be home. Goodall was a real good pilot.

It was 1st Lieutenant Goodall's last mission. The reason Hyde was flying with Douglas Richards' crew was that it was Goodall's last mission, and Hyde liked to fly with men on their last mission, and he also liked Goodall. At first men had to complete 50 missions before they could be sent home, but later it was cut down to 35 missions. Few men would have gotten out alive if it had been kept at 50.

Goodall's plane got a direct flak hit and blew up in a ball of flame, as I had seen happen over Ploesti. They blew up right off my right wing as I was sitting there, and I could watch them. You would think that not one person would ever get out alive. This was not the case. The tail turret gunner, Litcher, a fellow from Syracuse, NY, who had been my tail turret gunner for many months, back in Muroc, etc., was blown out of the airplane. His chute was burned open, and he was severely burned but landed alive and was taken care of in the German hospitals. He spent months and months getting skin surgery on his face and other parts of his body in a hospital in Valley Forge when he returned after the war was over. Litcher wrote or told me that. Hyde got out of it alive, and I saw him for the first time since the war at the bomb group reunion in Arizona in 1991.

When Goodall's plane was hit, Thompson fell through the bomb bay. One door had stuck open. He had a backpack chute that opened. On the ground, Hyde administered first aid to him because of his bleeding by putting on a tourniquet. He died that night in a hospital.

Hyde's chute was torn open. After being on the ground for several hours, a German tried to kill Hyde. Hyde was in prison camp at Stalag III. He left Stalag III to go to Nuremberg and then on April 4, he was marched to Moosberg.

Hyde said there were only 4 backpack chutes in the squadron at the time of the Blechhammer raid. The four who had them were: Wes Hyde, John Litcher, Robert Thompson, and myself.

There were two kinds of parachutes. One was the backpack kind that a man already had on in the plane. The other kind was what everyone had if he didn't have the backpack kind. This kind had a harness which had two rings on your chest; the chute was packed in a 18″ long x 9″ wide cylinder. This was picked off the floor of the airplane and snapped on when needed. It was impossible to wear this kind and work in the plane at the same time. For instance, all your turret gunners would have left the chute outside of their turrets and would have to get out of the turret and snap it on. The ball turret gunner would be in the turret hanging below the airplane, and his chute would be above on the floor of the airplane.

One time the bombardier, Curran, had his chute fall out through the nose wheel hole on takeoff and instead of telling me to abort the mission, we went on the mission. I didn't know Curran had lost his chute until the mission had finished. If I had known and if the plane had been seriously damaged, I would have tried to land the plane to save Curran since he didn't have his chute rather than have everyone bail out.

When Captain Hyde and my crew were shot down over Blechhammer, I remember that Hyde left a bottle of Haig and Haigh Pinch scotch. This is a premium Scotch, and Sam Parks, the squadron CO, took that. It goes to show that you never want to keep anything very valuable around your tent.

Three members of my crew that I had had since Gowen Field, Idaho, were killed on this bomb run: Goodall, Thompson, and Rich. Curran, Krenek, Shields, Brown, and Nickel had already gone home to the USA, because they had completed their number of missions. Litcher (of the original crew) was taken prisoner. Captain Hyde was the only other person to get out alive, but he was not part of my original crew.

For a more detailed description of the Blechhammer mission of August 22, 1944, see "Chapter VII: Gail Downs Interview with Wes Hyde" on page 147.

Our plane, at the same time Goody was blown out of the sky, was hit severely. We lost two engines, one on each side, otherwise we couldn't fly any length of time. We also lost much fuel. We immediately descended to 10,000 feet, and orders were given to the crew to throw out all our ammunition, machine guns, any waist guns we could get off, flak suits, and anything else of weight. We headed back to Italy. We flew across Czechoslovakia, Hungary (or maybe it was Austria), and then into Yugoslavia. I kept calling the navigator for estimated time of arrival for Vis. This was a little island off the coast of Yugoslavia, right off from Split.

The partisans, Tito's forces, held Vis. They were friendly to our troops. Vis had a little, short runway about 1,500 feet long. It was set in a valley. As I checked with the navigator, we realized our ground speed was about 110 MPH. We had a head wind and I don't remember the air speed. We would normally fly at about 165 MPH ground speed. We were going really slow, and it seemed like an eternity to ever get to the island of Vis. The mountains of Yugoslavia extend upwards of 10,000 feet and we weren't much higher. We weren't on oxygen. As we went across the country, we didn't see any enemy aircraft. Not one ever came up towards us, and had we seen any, I had given instructions to bail out. We didn't intend to sit there like sitting ducks.

The island was out of sight of land, perhaps 30 to 40 miles out. It was a dirt runway, graveled dirt or sand, and it went downhill as we landed. We landed hot, as we only had two engines. There was a mountain at the end of the runway, so our first time in was our only time, and we made sure we would get to the runway. We landed the airplane very fast. As soon as we hit the end of the runway, we locked the brakes, and the airplane slid the length of the runway. As we pulled over to the side, we were out of gas. We couldn't run the engines to taxi back to where they were keeping the airplanes. There were several airplanes that came in that day. They were never flown out but just landed and left there. I remember asking a partisan right away for a drink of water. He had wine in his canteen. At least it was wet. We stayed that night with the partisans in a big cement building, and next morning a C-47 or DC-3, that type of aircraft, came in from Bari, Italy, and flew us back to Bari and then back to our squadron and work and other missions. All the airplanes were from the Blechhammer trip of that day and previous missions. I suppose they were cut up for junk.

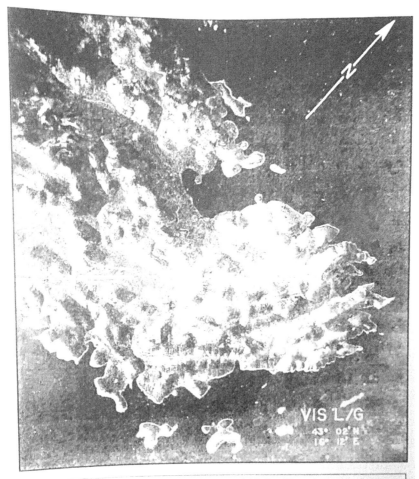

Vis was a mountainous island in the Eastern Adriatic. The emergency strip was long enough to land a B-24, but not long enough for a take-off. It saved crews who could not get back over the Adriatic to Italy.

I'm amazed when we go to these bomb group reunions 40 years later, how many people there were shot down or were prisoners of war or escapees and got out alive. In the reunion in Fort Worth in May 1989, Don Manlove was there. He was shot down, but I think his whole crew came back. This was the first time I had seen him since 1944. Al Leonard was shot down over Ploesti. I think most of his crew came back. He's been coming to many of these reunions since the war. He wasn't at this one in Fort Worth.

FOR THE 346TH BOMB SQUADRON THE 22ND OF AUGUST WAS A VERY BAD DAY INDEED. THE TARGET WAS BLECHHAMMER SOUTH SYNTHETIC OIL PLANT AND OVER THE TARGET A/C #256 RECEIVED DIRECT FLAK HIT IN THE LEFT WING AFTER THE RALLY FROM THE TARGET AND FLAMES STREAKED BACK THE LENGTH OF THE FUSELAGE. THE LEFT WING CRUMBLED AND THE SHIP FELL OFF TO THE LEFT AND TURNED OVER ON ITS BACK. FROM HERE ON THE ACCOUNTS DIFFERED. SOME SAY THE SHIP EXPLODED, OTHERS SAY IT CRASHED ON THE GROUND; SOME SAW NINE CHUTES OPEN, OTHERS DIDN'T SEE ANY. NEARLY ALL MEN ON THE THIS SHIP WERE ON THEIR 50TH MISSION AND CAPTAIN FREDERICK HYDE, 746TH OPERATIONS OFFICER WAS ALSO ABOARD. LATER, SGT. /HASS SAID, "OUR PLANE #018 WAS HIT BY A FLAK BURST AND #4 ENGINE AND THE HYDRAULIC SYSTEM WERE SHOT OUT. NEAR THE YUGOSLAVIAN COAST WE WERE GETTING LOW ON GAS AND ENGINES NUMBER 2 AND 3 WERE FEATHERED. THE ORDER TO BAIL OUT WAS GIVEN. LT. POUND, NAVIGATOR, JUMPED FIRST AND THE REST FOLLOWED. JUST BEFORE THE PILOT JUMPED THE PLANE LUNGED AND STARTED TO GO DOWN. ALL CREW MEMBERS EXCEPT LT. WOOD, PILOT; LT. POUND, NAVIGATOR AND SGT. STEELE WERE RESCUED BY A BRITISH COASTAL PATROL BOAT. LATER, THE CAPTAIN OF THE PATROL BOAT SAID THAT HE HAD SEEN THE LAST MAN OUT OF THE PLANE, PRESUMABLY LT. WOOD, FLOATING ABOUT FIFTY FEET BEHIND THE WRECKAGE. HE APPEARED TO BE ALRIGHT AND THE BOAT WENT TO THE REST TO PICK UP ANY INJURED MEN. WHEN THEY RETURNED, ONLY THE PARACHUTE WAS FLOATING. SEVERAL DAYS AFTERWARDS THE BODIES OF ALL THREE MEN WERE FOUND.

FROM THE 747TH BOMB SQUADRON WE LEARN THAT THE S-2 SHACK HAS BEEN REMODELED AND IS NOW BEDECKED WITH MAPS OF EVERY FRONT, AND NUMEROUS AIRCRAFT MODELS HANG FROM THE CEILING. THE TRAFFIC IN THE SHACK IS CONTINOUS, AND IT IS ESTIMATED THAT MORE THAN 250 MEN BROSE AROUND THE MAPS EVERY DAY. EVERYTHING IS DONE TO MAKE THE SHACK AS COMFORTABLE AS POSSIBLE. SOMETHING NEW HAS ALSO BEEN ADDED TO THE SQUADRON, A SOLID BRICK BUILDING WITH CEMENTED WALLS AND FLOORS AND 10 INDIVIDUAL SHOWERS; HOURS 1300 TO 1900.

SECRET

OFFICIAL SECRET

22 August 1944

<u>Stations</u>: 0650.   <u>Start engines</u>: 1st Box: 0700  2nd Box: 0710
                                                3rd Box: 0720

<u>Taxi out</u>: 0710.   <u>Take-off</u>: 0720

<u>Bomber Rendezvous</u>: Over STORNARA at 5000' at 0812- Ld. 455th 3rd.

<u>Cruising formation</u>: "VEE" of 9 ship Boxes.

<u>Bombing formation</u>: Column of Boxes.

| <u>Route</u>: | | | <u>Dist</u>. | <u>M. Crse</u> | <u>Alt</u>. | <u>ETR</u> |
|---|---|---|---|---|---|---|
| KPT | SCEDRO IS. | 4305/1642 | 111 | 25° | 14,000 | 0901 |
| | PITOMACA | 4557/1715 | 174 | 10° | | |
| | SARVAR | 4715/1655 | 78 | 352° | | |
| | HLOHOVEC | 4826/1748 | 80 | 028° | | |
| I.P. | TROPPAU | 4956/1755 | 94 | 04° | | |
| TGT. | BLECHHAMMER<br>South Oil Plant | 5018/1815 | 26 | 34° | 21,700 | 1110 |

Rally Left to 10° then left around ODERTAL to 5022/1752.

| | ODERLOGAU | 5022/1752 | | 250° | | |
|---|---|---|---|---|---|---|
| | HLOHOVEC | 4826/1748 | 117 | 183° | | |
| | SARVAR | 4715/1656 | 80 | 208° | | |
| | PITOMACA | 4557/1715 | 78 | 172° | | |
| | SCEDRO | 4305/1642 | 174 | 190° | | |
| | Base | | 111 | 205° | | |

<u>Fighter Rendezvous</u>:

<u>Window</u>:  2 cartons, 3 min before IP - 4 units/20 sec.

TARGETS:  <u>PRIMARY</u>:  BLECHHAMMER South (5018/1815). IP TROPPAU
          (4956/1755); Axis 34°M; Rally Left to 10° M; then
          left around ODERTAL.  Base Alt. 21,700 ft; Target
          Elev. 606; Intervalometer setting: 25 ft.
          <u>SECONDARY</u>:  BOHUMIN (4954/1821); IP DEUTSCH KRAWARN (4956/1801);
          Axis 99°M; Rally Right: Base Alt. 21,700 ft; Target
          Elev. 662; Intervalometer setting 25 ft.

<u>CALL SIGNS</u>:  456th: EXCEED TWO-THREE.  <u>FIGHTERS</u>: KIDDIES.  <u>Recall</u>: SWEATSHIRT.

| <u>Place</u> | <u>Radius</u> | <u>Place</u> | <u>Radius</u> |
|---|---|---|---|
| SPLIT | 7 | 4628/1635 | OBS |
| 4318/1701 | OBS | GYOR | 10 |
| 4349/1631 | OBS | BRATISLAVIA | 10 |
| SISAK | 6 | 4745/1808 | 7 |
| BANJA LUKA | OBS | 4950/1818 | 9 |
| 4627/1644 | 7 | 4958/1818 | |

C O N F I D E N T I A L

No. _5/_                    BATTLE ORDER

22 August 1944

1st Box

Formation Leader: Ladd, Ecker    AF 143
No. 3: Major      AP 365          Dep Leader: Toscelli, Chandler  AP 522
                                  No. 4: Claxton      AP 239
No. 6: Shoop      AP 393          No. 5: Gillman      AP 189
                                  No. 7: Cisena       AP 672
No. 9: List       AP 628          No. 8: Romeis       AP 569
                                  No. 10: Webster     AP 904

2nd Box

Leader: Hall                AP 889
No. 3: Kurtz      AP 135          Dep Leader: Goodall        AP 256
                                  No. 4: Otis         AP 089
No. 6: Shinners   AP 594          No. 5: Wood         AP 018
                                  No. 7; Smith        AP 480
No. 9: Dungvant   AP 107          No. 8: White        AP 839
                                  No. 10: Maupin      AP 265
                                  No. 11: Cerrotti    AP 345

3rd Box

Leader: Craddock            AP 403
No. 3: Blewitt    AP 689          Dep Leader: Dysinger     AP 407
                                  No. 4: Lock         AP 208
No. 6: Morris     AP 087          No. 5: Vogel        AP 623
                                  No. 7: Lumb         AP 148
No. 9: Rowe       AP 328          No. 8: Smith        AP 571
                                  No. 10: Ogden       AP 108
                                  No. 11: Le Vally, Col Russell  AP 964

SPARES: 744th Sqdn 057, 745th Sqdn 134, 746th Sqdn 199, 747th 051

Stations: 0650    Start engines: A 0700 B 0710 C 0720

Taxi out: 0710        Take-off: 0720

Call Signs: 456th: EXCEED TWO THREE

Fighters: KIDDIES

Recall: SWEATSHIRT

C O N F I D E N T I A L

456TH BG IN ITALY — When you list the heroes of the war in Europe,
don't leave off the name of 1st Lt. Wilson Goodall, a Liberator
bomber pilot who is still reported missing in action.

The story of his heroic action on a bombing mission over Blechhammer, Germany, last August, came to light the other day during a
"hangar session" between a couple of pilots who flew in other planes
on the same mission.

Lt. Goodall was flying his 50th combat mission that day, the
mission that would have wound up his tour in the Italian campaign.

"I remember the mission pretty clearly," said the one pilot, now
an operations officer at this base. "The flak was terrific. Lt.
Goodall's plane was catching plenty of hell, too, but he stayed in
position in the formation and completed the bombing run with the group."

"A few seconds after bombs away a direct hit struck Lt. Goodall's
plane in the wing section between the number one and two engines."

"The entire wing burst into flames, and you could tell by the
way the plane was bouncing around that he was fighting desperately to
keep the plane under control and on an even keel."

"He was cool though and saved us from a possible collision and
confusion by quickly pulling the plane out of the formation. Then,
we saw one, two, three chutes open."

"Almost immediately, the left wing broke into two pieces and
the plane, still burning, plunged toward the earth. We lost it in
the smoke and couldn't see if any more chutes opened or not, but when
last seen he was still trying to control the plane."

"He was a great pilot," the officer concluded, "but we haven't
heard a word of him since."

CONFIDENTIAL

PROPOSED CITATION

AWARD OF THE FIRST OAK LEAF CLUSTER (BRONZE) TO THE DISTINGUISHED FLYING CROSS

DOUGLAS C. RICHARDS, O-661129, Captain, 746th Bombardment Squadron, 456th Bombardment Group. For extraordinary achievement in aerial flight as pilot and leader of a flight of B-24 type aircraft. On 22 August 1944, Captain Richards led his flight on a bombing mission against the vital Blechhammer South Synthetic Oil Refinery, Germany. Despite intense and accurate anti-aircraft fire, a successful bombing run was made which greatly contributed to the grave damage inflicted upon the enemy installations. During the rally, a direct flak hit caused two (2) engines to be feathered, forcing the aircraft to leave the comparative safety of the formation. One (1) fuel tank was damaged and the mechanical failure of the booster pump to another made it impossible to transfer fuel. Captain Richards ordered all movable equipment jettisoned and through superb airmanship controlled the crippled plane, maintaining sufficient altitude to return across the mountains. Because the fuel supply was critical, it was necessary to consume a minimum of gasoline and fly a direct route to friendly territory. On approaching an advanced base a third engine began cutting out for lack of fuel. Displaying exceptional proficiency and cool judgment, he made a power-off landing without further damage to the plane or injury to the crew and thereby completed the difficult mission with a high degree of success. By his courage, professional skill, and faithful devotion to duty in the face of great opposition throughout thirty-five (35) successful sorties against the enemy, Captain Richards has reflected great credit upon himself and the Armed Forces of the United States of America. Residence at appointment: Lockport, New York.

CONFIDENTIAL

PROPOSED NARRATIVE

AWARD OF THE FIRST OAK LEAF CLUSTER (BRONZE) TO THE DISTINGUISHED FLYING CROSS

On 22 August 1944, Captain Douglas C. Richards was pilot and leader of a flight of B-24 type aircraft on a mission to bomb the vital Blechhammer South Synthetic Oil Refinery, Germany. Despite intense and accurate anti-aircraft fire in the target area, Captain Richards led his flight successfully through the bombing run to inflict grave damage on the enemy installations. During the rally, direct flak hits caused the number two (2) and the number four (4) engines to be feathered.

All movable equipment was immediately jettisoned, but the plane was unable to maintain sufficient flying speed and altitude to remain with the formation.

Because it was impossible to transfer fuel from the tanks of the damaged engines, it was imperative that Captain Richards conserve his fuel by flying the most direct route to the base. Mountainous peaks and enemy flak positions added to the already hazardous return trip, and it was only because of superior airmanship that the aircraft, deep behind enemy lines, could be guided to safety.

While still one (1) hour and thirty (30) minutes from the nearest base, oil pressure on the number three (3) engine began to drop. With an indicated oil pressure of forty (40) pounds in the number three (3) engine, Captain Richards landed his crippled aircraft without power. It was found that the number three (3) fuel tank had been completely drained, and the number one (1) tank contained but fifty (50) gallons.

A high degree of professional skill, cool judgment, and courage on the part of Captain Richards resulted in the safe return of this aircraft and its crew.

CONFIDENTIAL

# CHAPTER VI:
# REST & RECREATION TRIPS

*R&R destinations for Douglas Richards.*
*Map by grandson David Godfrey.*

It seems like it didn't take much to make us laugh over there. I can remember one time that Dan Curran was saving all of his beer cans in the tent. He lined up all his cans along the side of the tent in the shape of a pyramid or piled them on top of one another. One day we came in and drank all his beer and then set the cans back up the way they were. He didn't appreciate it very much. This was at Cerignola.

We had the good fortune to go to Cairo at least twice for a week at a time. These were our rest and recreation (R&R) trips. The first time we flew in for a week and then returned. They converted one of the B-24s, took the turrets off and that sort of thing so we could fly. It wasn't really a passenger ship. There were only two seats, three with the seat for the Radio Operator. The rest would sit on the floor or wherever. Cairo is a fascinating city. We were able to tour the big museum where King Tut lies and also the Shepheard's Hotel and the Men's Bar. We had loads of time to look them over. This hotel was world famous and at the crossroads of the Middle East for many years.

*Cairo, Egypt, December 1944. Air entrance to Cairo, Nile River.*

*Cairo, Egypt, December 1944. Gardens, Capt Elmore (front);*
*(back, L to R) Elmore's crew navigator (Lt), Capt Curran, bombardier.*

*Egypt, December 1944. Pyramid, Douglas*
*C Richards riding a camel.*

One time we had several guys from Group. We had the Group Major, a doctor, flight surgeon, and the Group Intelligence Officer, Captain Smith, and others. I don't remember who my copilot was. We flew into Cairo and got tired of that, so we flew to Tel Aviv, Israel, and spent a week over there. This was late in 1944 or early 1945.

I remember that the flight surgeon hardly ever got out of the hotel or the barroom. The rest of us went into Jerusalem for a day on the back of a 6x6 truck. We spent the day touring Jerusalem, Bethlehem, and Mount of Olives. In Gethsemane I was carrying a camera. It was a little bomb camera that we would use to take pictures of where practice bombs hit. I didn't have any other camera, and I got some pretty good pictures. We would get the film from Group and have it developed at Group too. The pictures of the pyramids and the Sphinx were taken with that camera from the airplane on the way back into Cairo.

*Palestine, December 1944. Garden of Gethsemane, Douglas C Richards.*

*Palestine, December 1944. Mount of Ascension*
*(L to R) Capt. Smith, Douglas Richards.*

*Palestine, December 1944. On road to Bethlehem.*

*Palestine, December 1944. Wailing Wall.*

JERUSALEM
THE WESTERN WALL (WAILING WALL).
(Lam. i. 4 - 11.)

It is a remainder of the wall that surrounded
the Temple area built by Herod I. This relic
is the only remains of the ancient glory that
stood on "Mount Moriah" and is looked upon,
as the most sacred place to the Jewish people.

*Palestine, December 1944. Garden of Gethsemane,*
*Jesuit mission, on way from Cairo.*

*Cairo, Egypt, December 1944. Air entrance to Cairo.*

It was interesting going into Tel Aviv. We loaded that B-24 bomb bay up with all those good grapefruit and oranges from Israel and flew them back to our base in Italy. We had to go back to Cairo and then fly from there to Foggia.

When we got back to Cairo, we picked up two Air Force nurses, who were on recreation leave in Cairo, and we took them back with us to Italy. They are in one of the pictures. Their job was to fly the wounded back from Africa to the USA. When we arrived at Cerignola, the Group fellows took them up to Group Headquarters, and Colonel Steed and General Upthegrove didn't know what to do with them. The whole thing was a big mess because they had to get these girls back to Africa to go to work. Here they were with a bomber group in Italy. I didn't dare go near Group operations for a week after that, but then it cooled off, and no one ever heard anything about it. That was just one of those things that happened.

*Cairo, Egypt, December 1944. Air evacuee nurses who flew to Italy with Group crew, then had to be flown back to Cairo.*

*Cairo, Egypt, December 1944. Air evacuee nurses with*
*Capt Smith, Group Intelligence, our Group plane.*

My wife Mina and I went back to Italy and took the ferry from Pescara to Split, which is the main city in Yugoslavia that you would pass in the flight from Italy going to Ploesti. We couldn't go to Vis. This was my idea, but it is now an army base, and we were not allowed to make the trip. We enjoyed the hospitality and spent a couple of nights in Split. It wasn't like being home, but it was country we had flown over many, many times.

We knew they had some guns, but we always stayed clear of those on the way in or across Yugoslavia. Everyone remembers Split if they flew out of the Adriatic.

I want to mention the citations listed at the bottom. There may be others that aren't listed. We used to say they were given out with the K-rations. They were to boost our morale, no doubt, but we really took them with a grain of salt. The write-ups were a bit flowery and exaggerated, etc. The newspapers listed our awards and ribbons that we had won.

ALL SQUADRONS ARE NOW ORGANIZED INTO FLIGHTS AND MANY IMPROVEMENTS HAVE BEEN NOTED. FOR A TYPICAL EXAMPLE OF THIS TYPE SET-UP SEE THE ORGANIZATIONAL PLAN OF THE 747TH SQUADRON AT THE END OF THE NARRATIVE SECTION.

 WITH THE ANNOUNCEMENT OF THE AWARD OF THE FIRST OAK LEAF CLUSTER TO THE ⟵ DISTINGUISHED FLYING CROSS, CAPTAIN DOUGLAS C. RICHARDS CREW BECAME ONE OF THE MOST DECORATED CREWS OF THE 746TH SQUADRON, PAST OR PRESENT. THE CREW COLLECTIVELY HOLDS THREE SILVER STARS, THREE DISTINGUISHED FLYING CROSSES AND FOUR PURPLE HEARTS.

1ST LT. THOMAS J. ANTHANASSION RETURNED TO THE 747TH SQUADRON, 10 DECEMBER 1944, AFTER ESCAPING INTERNMENT IN SWITZERLAND. LT. ANTHANASSION WAS A LEAD SQUADRON BOMBARDIER AND WAS INTERNED AFTER BAILING OUT OVER LAKE CONSTANCE. HIS SQUADRON ALONG WITH THE REST OF THE GROUP BOMBED AN AIRCRAFT FACTORY IN FRIEDRICHSHAFEN, GERMANY.

BOTH CHRISTMAS AND NEW YEAR'S DAY WERE CELEBRATED BY PARTIES AND TURKEY DINNERS. SECOND AND EVEN THIRD PORTIONS WERE GIVEN OUT AND EVERY MAN LEFT THE TABLE "FILLED TO THE GILLS". MESS HALLS AND CLUBS WERE COMPLETELY DECORATED WITH HOLLY, CHRISTMAS TREES, TINSEL AND EVEN ARTIFICIAL SNOW.

UNEXPECTEDLY, ON THE LAST DAY OF THE YEAR WE HAD OUR FIRST SNOW FALL. THE FLAKES WERE LARGE AND SWERVED ABOUT IN REAL "CHRISTMAS CARD STYLE".

LT. CHESTER A. PALKA RECENTLY RETURNED FROM THE FRONT LINES TO THE 747TH SQUADRON AFTER ACTING AS A LAISON OFFICER. HE BROUGHT BACK SEVERAL INTERESTING SOUVENIRS WHICH WERE DISPLAYED IN THE SQUADRON S-2 BUILDING.

SECRET

INCLUDED IN THIS DISPLAY WAS A GERMAN STOVE USED BY THE FIRST LINE TROOPS, A GERMAN PARATROOPERS RAPID FIRING RIFLE AND MANY PROPAGANDA LEAFLETS.

The pictures show General Arnold, General Nat Twining, and General Upthegrove. General Arnold was head of the Air Force, a five-star general. General Twining was the 15th Air Force commander, and General Upthegrove was commander of the 304th Wing. Colonel Steed was our Group Commander. You will see their pictures in the book. This was quite an honor for our squadron. We looked forward to the visit from so much brass. One page shows Captain Mueller, who was a Squadron Bombardier when I was the Operations Officer.

*Cerignola, Italy, 1945. Formation to meet Gen Hap Arnold. Lt Col Sam Parks meeting Gen Arnold, Maj Ken Bryant, as Douglas Richards nervously watches.*

*Cerignola, Italy, 1945. Gen Arnold, Col Steed arriving at squadron.*

*Cerignola, Italy, 1945. Group HQ inspection trip, coming out
of operations door. Col Steed, Gen Arnold, Gen Twining.*

*Cerignola, Italy, 1945.Group HQ inspection trip: Gen Upthegrove (304th Wing), Gen Twining (15th AF), Gen Arnold (AAF), Col Steed (456th BG).*

*Cerignola, Italy, April 26, 1945. Inspection in "A" Flight Room during bombardier and navigator training class
(left to right), Col. Steed; Gen. Arnold; Lt. Nelson, Lead
Bombardier, 746th Squadron; Brig. Gen. Upthegrove (riding
crop or baton denotes authority); Maj. Gen. Twining; Maj.
Richards; and Lt. Col. Parks, 746th Squadron Commander.*

*Cerignola, Italy, 1945. Capt Mueller, Squadron Bombardier.*

There is a picture of Royal Elmore, who was a good friend of mine and a good pilot. He would fly those missions when they were clouded over, and they would bomb by radar just to keep the enemy off balance.

*Cerignola, Italy, 1945. Capt Royal Elmore, Pilot and Flight Leader.*

Capt Royal Elmore and his copilot & their airplane.
    ↓
  on left

74th Squadron Operations Office, Stewart Field
Doug Richards on right
1943

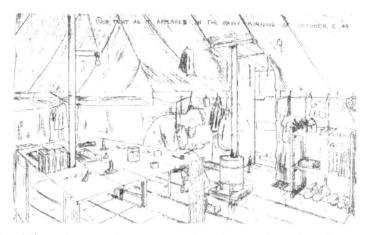

*Royal Elmore's tent as it appears on the rainy morning of October 5, 1944. Cots, footlocker, stove—was at ridge post in middle of tent. This tent is a lot nicer than mine because it has table, bookcase.*

*Elmore was a lead pilot (746th) so had group navigator with him. Royal bombed Berschtesgaden—Hitler's retreat in Bavarian Alps. Royal's drawing of his tent in Italy. He was D. Richards' assistant operational officer at one time. "Mickey Mission" was to bomb all alone, one plane only, by radar at night to keep the Germans on edge 24 hours a day.*

I can tell you about Louis Trippi. He was a captain and our squadron's flight surgeon. I'm sure everyone in our squadron could tell you about him. He was an obstetrician by trade. To keep in practice, he would go out and deliver a few Italian babies. This was against regulations, but sometimes we didn't worry about regulations, especially when they didn't affect anybody. Trippi, being a doctor, was highly respected in Italy, and it was an honor for him to deliver someone's baby in Italy. He wouldn't go to the hospital to deliver the baby. I'm sure they wouldn't let him.

One time we took Trippi on a flight to Bari. We got Trippi in the airplane. He didn't fly that much. We feathered one engine (shut the engine down and stopped the prop from turning), and pretty soon we feathered another engine. (So we would feather two engines at the same time. There were two more engines going.) Then we hollered at Trippi to scare him a little bit. He was a very conscientious doctor, even though doctors normally didn't like serving in the service because they weren't doing what they were trained to do. His main duty was to take care of sore throats and so on. He trained his staff sergeant to be head of the clinic and to do all of his work. The staff sergeant became a doctor after the war.

When we got home, Trippi served as our obstetrician when our two children were born. Trippi was from Buffalo, NY, and we lived about 45 miles from there. I have fond memories of Trippi. He died in 1986 of cancer, I think. He was a nice guy.

The first time I went to Rome was by jeep. I have several pictures of this trip. When Mina and I went to Italy the first time, many years ago, we went into the Vatican in St. Peter's Square. I expected to be the only one there. During the war, we were the only tourists in town, and I expected the same treatment twenty years later. This time it was mobbed, and so I look back to the time when it wasn't so full of tourists. One picture shows all of St. Peter's Square. Not many troops were in that square. We had a private audience with Pope Pius. It was probably on the second floor of the Vatican, in a room that held perhaps one or two thousand people. They carried the Pope in on his litter. He went down the rows and blessed us all. Rome was an impressive place, and we enjoyed taking leave there. I flew into Rome and spent a week at a time, several times.

*Rome, Italy, 1944. Colosseum, Douglas C Richards.*

*Rome, Italy, 1944. Colosseum, Lt Curran, Lt Enderbo, Lt Emery.*

*Rome, Italy, 1944. Mussolini's balcony where he made his speeches.*

*Rome, Italy, 1944. Mussolini's Square, photo taken
from Victor Emmanuel Monument.*

*Rome, Italy, 1944. Vatican, photo taken from St Peter's Basilica.*

*Rome, Italy, 1944. Vatican, St Peter's, Douglas C Richards and other soldiers had private audience with Pope Pius here.*

*Rome, Italy, 1944. Vatican, St Peter's, Douglas Richards.*

*Rome, Italy, 1944. Vatican, St Peter's, Lt Jones.*

*Rome, Italy, 1944. Victor Emmanuel Monument in front of Forum.*

When we first got into Italy, they had a place in Capri where our crew could go. We went although we didn't need leave from combat at that time. Our crew stayed with other officers at Anacapri. Mina and I, on our trip in 1983, went to Anacapri. We were staying on Amalfi Drive at Positana, and we went over to Capri by boat. We went to Anacapri to see the hotel where we stayed during the war. I recognized the hotel, but they had turned it into an apartment house. They had a restaurant on the first floor, and the bar was still there. We had a nice lunch out on the terrace. During the war, we were there in February, so couldn't eat on the terrace, but I remember looking up to see the palm trees and all the vegetation. It brought back memories of the week we spent there.

In Capri we were the tourists, and we could ride from Capri to Anacapri. They didn't allow cars, so we went up by donkey or a cart with a donkey pulling it. We went up and saw the castle of Tiberius, and we also had the boatman row us into the Blue Grotto. Mina and I did the same thing, having the man row us there. At that time they had a police boat acting as a traffic cop. We had to take turns. In 1944 we didn't have to put up with that. We were IT at that time.

Boats to row to go to Blue Grotto. Picture to Doug Richards from Capt. Kay "Elmore" pilot

I have several pictures of northern Italy. Capt. Elmore and I made this trip at the close of the war. The war had wound down. I was Operations Officer, and he was my assistant. We didn't have anything to do. Col. Parks was Commanding Officer of the squadron, and we wrote out fictitious orders, not that we really needed them. We planned to spend a week or more in northern Italy. V-E Day had not happened yet. We celebrated V-E Day (May 8, 1945) while we were at Lake Como.

The ride up the Adriatic in our jeep was the way to travel. We were the only ones that were traveling. As you can see by the pictures, there was not a railroad bridge or a road bridge or any other kind standing at the end of the war. Our fighter-bombers and B-25s had done a thorough job of destroying every bridge in northern Italy. We used Bailey bridges, which are metal bridges, like an erector set bridge, between Cerignola and Foggia during the war. Our troops had bombed that out. The Bailey bridge is a very efficient bridge, and the engineers had put them up.

We drove up the Adriatic, passing Rimini, where we had bombed, and then went up the Po River to Bologna. The Group bombed the marshalling yard (for freight trains) in that city. We stayed the first night with British troops in a large building on the second floor. There were lots of cots. We awakened in the morning and were served tea. This was the first time in my life I had been served tea in bed.

*Italy, 1944–45. Maj. Bryant, Squadron Executive*
*Officer; Lt. Col. Parks, Commanding Officer.*

*Italy, Po Valley May 1945. Bailey bridge. Not a bridge was standing in northern Italy.*

*Italy, Po Valley May 1945. Bologna.*

We proceeded up the Po River. We finally came to a pontoon bridge. At the time, there were German prisoners walking back, you might say unattended, towards us, coming from the front. They were also in trucks going back to our rear. It was dusty. To my knowledge, this was the only bridge across the Po River. This was the route to Milan. From here you could go to Genoa or Verona or Venice. We crossed here to Milan and had no problems in getting a hotel. They accepted our invasion currency, and we spent a few nights there.

*Italy, Po Valley May 1945. German prisoners*
*walking toward us on pontoon bridge.*

*Italy, Po Valley May 1945. Po River, crossing pontoon bridge on way to Milan.*

*Italy, Po Valley May 1945. Armistice.*

*Italy, Po Valley May 1945. Betsy (our jeep) and Capt Royal Elmore.*

*Italy, Po Valley May 1945. Bomb damage.*

*Italy, Po Valley May 1945. Bombed apartment houses.*

*Italy, Po Valley May 1945. British Universal Carrier.*

*Italy, Po Valley May 1945. British troops.*

*Italy, Po Valley May 1945. Church steeple.*

*Italy, Po Valley May 1945. More bomb damage.*

*Italy, Po Valley May 1945. Po Valley Road trip taken by Capt Elmore, Ass't Operations Officer, and Maj Douglas Richards, Operations Officer.*

*Italy, Po Valley May 1945. Railroad bridge bombed with a train on it.*

*Italy, Po Valley May 1945. Tank park; Betsy (our jeep) needed a spark plug change.*

*Italy, Po Valley May 1945. Tank park; our two-cylinder jeep needed a spark plug change.*

*Italy, Po Valley May 1945*

*Italy, Po Valley May 1945. Verona, towers.*

*Italy, Po Valley May 1945. Adriatic coast line.*

*Italy, Po Valley May 1945. Ancona, Adriatic point of
German line for long period while in Italy.*

*Italy, Po Valley May 1945. Bologna, another view.*

*Italy, Po Valley May 1945. Bomb damage at Bologna.*

*Italy, Po Valley May 1945. British troops outside Ancona, Po Valley Road.*

*Italy, Po Valley May 1945. Entrance to Ancona.*

*Italy, Po Valley May 1945. More bomb damage at Bologna.*

Royal had a Rolleicord or Rolleiflex camera, which is a very famous camera, and he was an expert photographer. We had excellent pictures of this trip. He could develop them. I believe it was Capt. Mitchell who ran the Group photo department, and we had use of the photo lab where we could process film on US government paper. (I've seen Mitchell at our reunions in 1988 and 1989.) This enabled me to have a good pictorial record of the trip. The picture of the Milan cathedral, noted for its Gothic architecture, is beautiful.

*Italy, Po Valley trip, May 1945. Milan Cathedral, full view.*

Mussolini was captured and killed (April 28, 1945) on the far side of Lake Como and then hung up in front of the railroad station in the center of Milan. There is a picture in the book of this station. We were staying not far from the station, a couple of blocks away. It also shows a picture of the partisans or whatever they were called. It shows their picture where they are commemorating the end of the war and the death of Mussolini. We were in Milan about four or five days after Mussolini was killed.

*Italy, Po Valley trip, May 1945. Milan railroad
station, where Mussolini was hanged.*

*Italy, Po Valley trip, May 1945. Milan Cathedral, partisans
gathering in memory of partisans killed by Germans.*

*Italy, Po Valley trip, May 1945. Milan, main
building of town, shops, cafes, etc.*

*Italy, Po Valley trip, May 1945. Milan, part of hospital, jeep
of Richards and Elmore, inquiring about road to Como.*

*Italy, Po Valley trip, May 1945. Milan, truck off road.*

*Italy, Po Valley trip, May 1945. Pontoon bridge,
dusty road after crossing bridge.*

We went from Milan to Lake Como, and at the end of the lake is a lovely hotel. We were able to obtain the best room in the hotel, overlooking Lake Como. The room was probably 25 by 15 feet and cost us just a few dollars a day. We would go out and buy breakfast of meat and eggs. We were invited by an industrialist or manufacturer up to his villa or chalet in the mountains nearby.

*Italy, Po Valley trip, May 1945. Lake Como villa.*

While we were on Lake Como, we celebrated V-E Day. We had no news about it ahead of time. They had fireworks at night. This is a trip I will never forget. I would like to go back someday and show Mina Lake Como. It is beautiful country, but it will never be like we saw it, being the only tourists in town, no lines, everything was at our disposal for a very small amount of money. We spent only a few dollars a day to live there.

The only way we got gas was to pull into a British or American vehicle compound, and they would fill it up. On the way back, our spark plugs went bad. We pulled into a British place, and they repaired them for us. This was one of the fruits of victory after the war. We were probably the only ones who took this trip. Most people didn't have the opportunity to do it, nor did they think of it.

George Penhiman of the 747 squadron was an armament man. He was friendly with one of our people in our squadron. He came to me at war's end and said he wanted to go to northern Italy. I told him (I was operations officer) to get on this plane with food that was on the line (where airplanes are parked was called the line) before dawn. It was flying to northern Italy as a relief plane. Get off the plane and no one will know. He hitchhiked to Venice, Verona, and Milan. Partisans were still shooting at German sympathizers in Milan. He came up to me at the Tucson, Arizona, reunion in 1991 and thanked me for helping him get on a plane.

About two or three weeks after my Lake Como trip, Trippi and I took the cruise ship, the Argentina, from Naples to New York City. The trip took about 10 days.

This goes to show that in war anything goes. I always said the service or being in the service was strictly a wartime deal and that I wanted no part of it during peacetime. Regulations didn't mean too much. We had a job to do, and we took it very seriously. As far as other things, we took them with a grain of salt. We did pretty much as we pleased within bounds. This made for a good atmosphere. This was a civilian service, not professional. We were there to do a job and that was it. We didn't like the parades and formations in peacetime.

### Pre-deployment timeline:

1940: Graduated from Syracuse University

Fall 1940–March 1941: Made shock absorbers at Houdaille Manufacturing Company in Buffalo, NY.

March 1941: To avoid draft, enlisted in Air Force. Inducted in Buffalo, New York. Took train to Camp Dix, New Jersey. Month or less at Camp Dix. Took train to Atlanta, GA (had my first taste of grits at Atlanta terminal.)

March 28–November 1941: Took the train to Selma, Alabama, Selma Air Force Base. Trained in how to use a shovel. Decided then to become a pilot, digging ditches wasn't for me.

November 1941: Went home on Louisville–Nashville train. Hunted for a week.

November 15, 1941: Took train to St. Louis and on to Fort Worth, Texas, Hicks Primary Flying School (cadet school), which was run by civilians. Flew PT-19s.

December 7, 1941: I was at Fort Worth for the weekend on Pearl Harbor Day.

January 15–March 14, 1942: Randolph Air Force Base, San Antonio, Texas, for basic pilot training in BT-13. John O'Neil from the Ridge Road, Gasport, NY, was here at same time.

March 15, 1942: Took advanced flight training in AT-6s at Brooks Air Force Base, San Antonio. While there I got jaundice and was hospitalized for a month.

July 3, 1942: Graduated Brooks Air Force Base as a 2nd Lieutenant and as pilot—obtained pilot wings. Grandpa and Grandma

Coulter, my parents, and Aunt Elizabeth Smith drove down for graduation.

July 3–August 11, 1942: Stayed on at Brooks Air Force Base as observer pilot. Flew observers around. Observation training to detect troop movement or artillery firing. These were lieutenants and other personnel.

August 12–October 30, 1942: Served in DeRidder, Louisiana, as observation pilot.

October 31, 1942–June 30, 1943: Flew tow targets for anti-aircraft guns in 5th Tow Target Squadron at Palacios, TX.

July 16–August 25, 1943: Hendricks Field, Sebring, Florida. Instructed in flying B-17s. I went home on train for leave.

Sept 16, 1943: Reported at Gowen Field, Boise, Idaho. Assigned to 746th Bomb Squadron, 456th Bomb Group, picked up crew at Boise.

The author became Captain, June 17, 1944; Squadron Operations Officer, August 23, 1944; Major, February 2, 1945.

R E S T R I C T E D
COMBAT MISSION DATA

456TH BG

NAME  Richards, Douglas C.          RANK  Major    ASN  0661129

DUTY  Pilot                          SQ. 746th Bomb (H)APO  520

| | DATE | GROUP MISS. | SOR-TIES | COMBAT TIME | TOT.COMB. TIME | TARGET | CLAIMS |
|---|---|---|---|---|---|---|---|
| 1944 | 2-10 | 1 | 1 | 3:45 | 3:45 | Grottaferrata | |
| | 2-22 | 3 | 2 | 6:50 | 10:35 | Sibenik | |
| | 3-15 | 12 | 3 | 3:15 | 13:50 | Cassino | |
| | 3-18 | 15 | 4 | 5:15 | 19:05 | Maniago Landing Ground | |
| | 3-22 | 17 | 5 | 5:55 | 25:00 | Rimini Bologna M/Y | |
| | 3-24 | 19 | 6 | 5:50 | 30:50 | Rimini M/Y | |
| | 3-26 | 20 | 7 | 6:30 | 37:20 | Maniago | |
| | 3-28 | 21 | 8 | 5:50 | 43:10 | Verona M/Y | |
| | 3-29 | 22 | 9 | 6:10 | 49:20 | Milan M/Y | |
| | 3-30 | 23 | 10 | 6:40 | 56:00 | Sophia | |
| | 4-12 | 29 | 11 | 6:05 | 62:05 | Bad Voslau | |
| | 4-16 | 32 | 12 | 5:45 | 67:50 | Turnu Severin | |
| | 4-17 | 33 | 13 | 5:15 | 73:05 | Sophia M/Y | |
| | 4-21 | 35 | 14 | 7:30 | 80:35 | Bucharest M/Y | |
| | 4-23 | 36 | 15 | 6:15 | 86:50 | Bad Voslau | |
| | 4-30 | 41 | 16 | 6:30 | 93:20 | Milan M/Y | |
| | 5-5 | 42 | 17 | 7:25 | 100:45 | Ploesti M/Y | |
| | 5-7 | 44 | 18 | 7:05 | 107:50 | Bucharest M/Y | |
| | 5-12 | 46 | 19 | 6:55 | 114:45 | Chiaveri | |
| | 5-18 | 49 | 20 | 7:45 | 122:30 | Ploesti Refinery | |
| | 5-24 | 52 | 21 | 6:30 | 129:00 | Munchendorf A/D | |
| | 6-9 | 65 | 22 | 6:55 | 135:55 | Munich | |
| | 6-13 | 66 | 23 | 4:20 | 140:13 | Ferrara A/D | |
| | 6-13 | 68 | 24 | 6:45 | 147:00 | Munich | |
| | 6-28 | 75 | 25 | 6:35 | 153:35 | Karlova A/D | |
| | 7-3 | 78 | 26 | 7:30 | 161:05 | Malaxa | |
| | 7-20 | 87 | 27 | 6:40 | 167:45 | Friedrichshafen | |
| | 7-27 | 91 | 28 | 5:45 | 173:30 | Budapest | |
| | 8-13 | 98 | 29 | 8:05 | 181:35 | Orange RR Bridge | |
| | 8-22 | 105 | 30 | 8:15 | 189:50 | Blechhammer | |
| | 8-28 | 110 | 31 | 5:45 | 195:35 | Avisio Viaduct | |
| | 9-3 | 114 | 32 | 6:00 | 201:35 | Szeged RR Bridge | |
| | 10-10 | 132 | 33 | 5:45 | 207:20 | S-Dona Bridge | |
| | 10-11 | 133 | 34 | 5:10 | 212:30 | Osterreichische motor Works | |
| | 10-13 | 135 | 35 | 5:50 | 218:20 | Blechhammer | |
| 1945 | 1-19 | 184 | 36 | 5:10 | 223:30 | AWARDS Brod RR Bridge | |

| AWARD | AUTHORITY | DATE |
|---|---|---|
| Air Medal | Hq, 15th AF, G.O. # 174 | 6 Apr 44 |
| 1st Oak Leaf Cluster, Bronze | Hq, 15th AF, G.O. # 1251 | 22 June 44 |
| 2nd Oak Leaf Cluster, Bronze | Hq, 15th AF, G.O. # 2309 | 4 Aug 44 |
| 3rd Oak Leaf Cluster, Bronze | Hq, 15th AF, G.O. # 2309 | 4 Aug 44 |
| 4th Oak Leaf Cluster, Bronze | Hq, 15th AF, G.O. # 3350 | 13 Sept 44 |
| Distinguished Flying Cross | Hq, 15th AF, G.O. # 842 | 4 June 44 |
| Cluster to DFC | Hq, 15th AF, G.O. # 4889 | 6 Dec 44 |
| Cluster To Pres. Citation | " " " G.O. # 3223 | 16 May |

456TH BG                    R E S T R I C T E D

# CHAPTER VII: GAIL DOWNS INTERVIEW WITH WES HYDE

An audio-tape interview with Wes Hyde was recorded on June 6th, 1992, at the 456th Bomb Group Reunion in Milwaukee, Wisconsin, and transcribed in April 1993, by Gail Elliott Downs (Thomas), relative of George Elliott Rich, radio operator on the Purple Shaft, who was killed in action on August 22, 1944. Wes Hyde was the co-pilot on the plane which exploded over Blechhammer, Germany, killing George and seven other crew members. There was also a video interview with Douglas C. Richards, Wes Hyde, Walter Krowal, and Gail Downs at the 456th Bomb Group Reunion in Italy, April 1993. The following account combines both of the Gail Downs interviews with Wes Hyde.

In June or July 1943, we reported to an airfield right outside of Orlando, Florida, for special training for Cadre. (Cadre is an outline of people from which you will build an organization.) Things were happening so fast all over the Air Corps. They had a hard time finding places for us. We were sent from there to McGloughlin, Nebraska. Then we went to Muroc. The first crew to report in was Doug Richards'. His crew was #1. We numbered them as they came in.

Q: That was the whole crew? Already put together?

A: Yes.

Q: Dan Curran, George Rich, Jerry Krenek were all there?

A: Yes, they were all together at Muroc. They had to be in their spaces. They all reported in in September. They had to complete their training, fly their airplane, protect it, defend it, wrap the bombs and all as a crew at Muroc. Muroc was a very active, experimental field. We saw aircraft we had not even heard about, such as the B-36.

We went from there to Hamilton Field, south of San Francisco to pick up our new airplanes. After that, we left for overseas. Some flew formation across the United States making two or three stops. Each squadron had seventeen airplanes but twenty-one crews. We put the members of the other four crews among the seventeen planes as additional passengers.

We got to West Palm Beach, Florida, where we got our orders to go overseas. That was the first time we found out where we were going. We were going to Italy instead of England.

Then we went down to Trinidad on December 23rd, just before Christmas. From there to [a base] in Brazil, which is located in the estuary of the Amazon River. Then we flew down to Natal. We were held up there for a long time. We spent Christmas Day there.

We left Natal for Dakar, Senegal, in West Africa. Then from there to Marrakech, Morocco, in North Africa, then to Tunis. We waited in Tunis until we got word that the runways and hard stands had been completed at the airfield where we were assigned.

Q: All along, were you always 15th Air Force?

A: Yes, we became part of the 15th Air Force after we got over there.

Q: Did you do any bombing runs while in North Africa?

A: No. We flew and practiced formations there. Then we got up to Italy, Stornara, near Cerignola. We started our runs. We got there in January and the first mission we flew was over the beachhead near Grottaferrata, Italy, in early February, as I recall. I've not looked at a diary, but that's as I remember.

I didn't fly with Richards' crew very often, just when it was necessary for the books, for the records, as he was a totally qualified pilot with an outstanding crew. All were well qualified.

[2:40 on tape. Talks about 456th aircraft explosions, booby traps, losing crews… very difficult to hear.]

I made it clear to my crews that were finishing that I as their commander would fly with them on their next to last mission. So, whenever a crew reached 48 or 49 missions, I'd check the airplane myself and I'd go with that crew.

And on those days, I had another reason. Overall, they would be squeamish as they approached their 50th mission. They would be nervous, squeamish. Although they've survived this far, if you look at it either way, the odds say you're not going to make it through; but then the odds say, if you've made it this far, chances are you're going to complete it.

So, I tried to get my missions out of the way. As commander, I was only supposed to fly one out of every four missions because I was part of staff leadership. Doug and I weren't allowed to fly on the same mission. They didn't want to lose both of us at the same place.

So, I had flown four in a row, and we lost one airplane that day. Doug's crew flew on that mission too, with Richards' co-pilot as pilot. Richards was to be on the ground whenever I flew because he was my Assistant Operations Officer. Doug's crew completed their 49th mission, and I had planned to spend the next five days in Rome. We had just liberated Rome, and remember, it was a Free City. We never attacked Rome.

So that afternoon, which would be the 21st of August, after the missions were in and we knew what had happened, crews went through interrogation. I had just finished interrogation. Suddenly,

Goodall appears in the Operations tent and said, "Captain, the crew has sent me to ask you to take us on our last mission."

I said, "When do you want to go, Goody?"

He said, "Whenever you say, Sir."

I said, "Let's go tomorrow. Let's get it over with." I couldn't go to Rome for five days and let them sit on their duffs getting scared and squeamish.

I knew Doug's crew better than any other crew in the squadron because his crew was at Muroc first.

Another point I should have made earlier somewhere, is that early in the combat experience, I think it was Goodall that went to Richards and told Richards he had a premonition that he would not make it. This was early, probably in March, after their first five missions. This was before they started receiving those heavy crew losses. They did have more crew decorations than any other crew had. (Rich: 1 Purple Heart; Krenek: 3 Purple Hearts; cameraman: killed). That's just the luck of the draw. They just happened to be in the area of the flak when it went off. Almost all the flak we experienced was barrage fire. Doug told me about Goodall's premonition. Goody and I had not talked about Goody's premonition.

When we were issued our personal equipment, each squadron was issued four backpack chutes, as opposed to the chest packs. They were strapped and fitted around your back and shoulders so you could work around the airplane and not be out of your chute. You had the chute with you at all times.

There were only four backpacks for the squadron. They were assigned traditionally for the use of the four senior flying people: Squadron Commander, Squadron Operations Officer (me), Squadron Bombardier, and the Squadron Navigator.

But when we got to combat, we all put the chutes together in one tent. Those backpacks went to whomever, or whichever of the leadership was flying that day. If there was still one, two, or three remaining, then the crews who were first in line to get parachutes got the backpacks that were there – out of the four. Lehner had one of them the day he was shot down over Ploesti.

The day I flew with them, the 22nd, I took my backpack, the navigator Thompson took another backpack, and Litcher, the tail gunner, was in line early enough that he got one and Richards had the fourth one. The rest had chest packs. The chest packs clamp on rings.

Q: Was it because that crew was on their last mission that they got the backpacks?

A: No, but they had rank because of me.

Q: Were three backpacks on your plane because you were the highest-ranking officer?

A: One backpack was not on my plane. Richards had that one. I took mine. None of the other officers to whom those chutes had been assigned were flying that day. So the other two happened to end up on my plane by luck. The crew were in line early enough to get them; the tail gunner and the navigator.

In late June or July, Gutting lost his plane. It exploded for no apparent reason. I then announced that I would fly with people on their last mission. About a month before Blechhammer I recognized the blessing of backpacks.

As my flying and combat experience grew, I began to, of course, think about, "What if…" and "How am I going to get out?" And I had a premonition that I was going to face the exact experience that Goodall had feared… the fire and all. So I sat down and wrote a letter in May or June to my fiancée and told her about the backpack and that regardless of what she heard about my being missing in action, should that ever happen, don't give up hope because I probably got out of the airplane safely. She never gave up hope.

So, Goodall came to the tent and I said, "We're going tomorrow." He said, "Fine," and went out and told his crew. Of course, my office had to get to work right away and submit the crew names to fill in the holes. I told them who the pilot would be (Goodall). I would sit in the co-pilot seat. Goodall, on his last mission, would be in command. It was his crew. I made that my policy. The crew commander was in charge of his crew, not supervisory personnel along for the ride.

I went up after supper to Group headquarters for an evening briefing at which we were told what bomb loads we would carry, armament, when we would start engines, when we would taxi, when we would take off, the order we would fly in the formation, all that. The following morning, at the briefing for the entire crew, they would tell you about the mission.

The Group Navigator and I were standing together and he took me aside and said, "Are you going on a mission tomorrow?"

I said, "Yes", and told him why.

He said, "Don't go. Don't go." He talked to me for thirty minutes. We were good friends and he finally told me that the next morning I was going to be transferred to another squadron and placed in command of that squadron. I had been in command of my squadron and they brought in another officer from Group and put in him in command, so I went back to Operations and Doug went back to Assistant Operations. He told me some other things. He didn't tell me that my promotion (major) had come in and was there to be given to me that next day. The Army's procedure was if you were shot down before they pinned it on you, you didn't get it. I've forgotten the other arguments he expressed.

I said, "I promised the crew we're going tomorrow," which I had, of course. But finally, I said, "Tell me where we're going."

He said, "No, I can't tell you that."

I said, "You can draw a circle on the map showing me the general location." And he did. I said, "I've been up there a number of times, and it was always a milk run."

There was another reason that I set myself up to fly those last missions. I DID have an inordinate amount of good luck when I flew. We just didn't have accidents. We didn't generally even have flak. They were so far off our altitude that we suffered very little flak damage afterwards.

So, I prevailed and we took off. Doug was leading the squadron. He was flying in the right seat and in the left seat was a brand-new pilot, a captain who had never seen combat before. So, since he was a captain, I thought I had to check him out as a flight leader. So, Doug was showing him how to fly and lead the squadron in the position as the squadron's leader.

The diagram below illustrates "boxes" and usual flying patterns. It was an 11-man flight to Blechhammer.

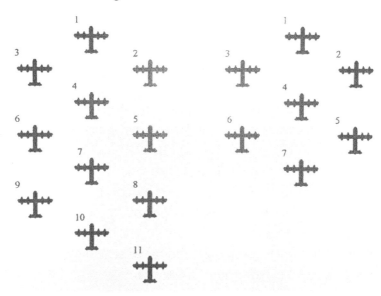

*1: Hall/Richards; 2: Goodall/Hyde; 3: Kurtz; 4: Otis; 5: Wood; 6: Shinnors; 7: Smith; 8: White; 9: Dunvannt; 10: Maupin; 11: Cerretti*

We bombed based on the leadership. When the leader's bombs went away, ours went away. When the leader's bombs went away, the lead bombardier was correcting for his course and speed. The bombardiers of the other boxes set the rate so that they would drop their bombs at the same point that the lead bombs went away. The lead bombardier flew the course, and we flew formation in that box.

Doug was leading the high right box, and I was on Goodall's (Doug's) crew. We were on the right wing looking at Doug all the way. As we approached the initial point, which is the point on the map from which you start your bomb run, I reached down for some reason and broke a long-standing practice: I put my seatbelt on. Normally, we took them off after take-off and never used them again until we got in a traffic pattern. I usually unhooked my seatbelt so I could react quickly and get out. I was being led to do something I didn't plan to do. I began to get serious about this mission about this time. So, as we started the bomb run, I reached down and put my seatbelt on, and I knew I was doing something I'd never done before, but I did it anyway. I felt a strange feeling that something else was moving me and making me… really, this is true… and I'm not coloring it either… this is exactly what happened.

I didn't think anything more about it. I was too busy watching and seeing what was going on. Everybody was approaching the target and looking for flak. We did have 88mm flak barrage fire over our target, Blechhammer South. Just to the southwest of us, Odertal, another major place we bombed, was being hit by another wing. Shortly after we dropped ours, they dropped theirs and got out of the way.

We were briefed to drop ours and make an immediate left turn at 5 degrees and fly for about fifteen minutes. Then start a slow turn back toward the base. The practice had been that the man in the right seat would take over for the man in the left seat after bombs went away, give him a rest. So, I said, "I've got it," and took over flying.

I said over the intercom, "Another milk run."

Litcher said, "It's not over till it's over," or words to that effect. Then everything got quiet.

All of a sudden, Ladd, the Group Operations Officer and leader of the Blechhammer mission, took us into a hard left turn (135 degrees) and a dive, all the way down to 17,000 feet from 24,500 feet. We were flying a much different course than we were supposed to be flying. That put our squadron, our bombers, our box, over Odertal, an oil refinery, to the immediate west of Blechhammer. Its guns were still hot, its crew was still on their guns because another wing had just finished bombing it.

I didn't know at the time and neither did our intelligence know because we'd already had our briefing, that a brand new, newly commissioned German gun, a railroad gun, 150 millimeters, was at Odertal. It aimed and fired and the first stick of eight shells came up on my right rear and took off the tip of the right wing. These were gigantic bursts that I'd never seen before; higher than this room is high, much higher than the ceiling. I could hear them explode; they were that loud. What I didn't know was that another stick came up on the left side. The first one of those that exploded near us hit the airplane at the root of the left wing, where the wing goes into the fuselage. It immediately burst into flames.

I was flying the airplane and Goody was resting after the bomb drop. I tightened up on Doug's wing. We were going down. I saw huge shells come up on the left. I turned to look at Doug. I thought I read what Doug was thinking. Goodall and I had not conversed with each other since right after the hit on the tip of the right wing. Then all of a sudden, we got that explosion at the root of the left wing. I said, "One hit the root of the left wing." The left wing started to fold away, and I watched it go. I watched Doug's eyes. I knew this was it. I worked the controls a little bit and nothing happened. Goodall left as soon as that shell exploded. The last thing I saw before I tried to stand up and go with him was his parachute, right there under his seat.

He never tried to pick up his chute when the plane was hit. He went towards the bomb bay.

Thompson was standing between the seats at the back, so I could always look over my shoulder where we were. Thompson dived for the bomb bay. He tried to get out through the bomb bay. One door had stuck open.

I first tried to get up several times and couldn't and was approaching panic. Then I remembered and undid the seatbelt. By then we were in a tight spin so the centrifugal force threw me up into the canopy (cockpit roof) with my feet towards the back and my head towards the nose.

I saw a great big hole in the windshield. I'd seen a B-17 co-pilot climb out with full gear, leather jacket, pants, the works. I'd actually seen him climb out of that window while the airplane was burning. So I said, "If he could do it, I could do it. I reached for that hole in the windshield, and I couldn't move my arms because of the centrifugal force. I looked down and I could see Germany spinning around down there and I stopped and prayed, "Dear God" and the plane exploded.

I felt a big shove. The next thing I was out, hanging in air, with my head to my chest. I've got to get my parachute open. I reached up to my flak helmet and my chin strap almost pulled my head off. I looked down, then looked up and there was the chute. I was blown out of the plane. I saw pieces of airplane fluttering, tumbling.

I looked down and saw one parachute apparently in good shape. I saw another parachute with holes in it way down below that had to be Litcher because it had burn holes in it, and he had a broken ankle.

When I got on the ground a German, national home-guard, greeted me and put a rifle on me and said, "Gehen Sie!" [Go!] I got to my feet and folded my parachute. This guy started marching me over to the woods when a noncombatant officer redirected the German. Then the noncombatant was busy and this guy started walking me to the woods again. I knew he was going to shoot me. Again, he was stopped and this time he took me to a shack. Thompson and Litcher were in the little shack.

Litcher was badly burned. Holes burned into his chute so he dropped at a much faster rate even though he was small. Thompson was bleeding very rapidly from his right knee. I proceeded to apply pressure and let up. I kept trying to keep the tourniquet on Thompson's leg. Thompson insisted that I loosen the tourniquet and not keep it on so long. I went through the motions to release the tourniquet. I did what I could do.

Litcher and I talked and two hours later in the afternoon while we were waiting to be taken to the hospital, Litcher wanted me to go over and get his ripcord so he could keep it. I said, "Litcher, don't be silly. You know you pulled that ripcord for the chute to be open."

Litcher said, "No, I didn't."

I said, "I didn't either." I handed it to him. As far as I know he still has it.

We know that Goodall left without his chute. Litcher or a German who spoke some English told me that Goodall's body was found wrapped around the engine. Litcher saw the other men standing still at their assigned locations unable to move. None of them reached for their chutes. The ball turret gunner was still in the turret. Litcher was extremely unhappy because he was able to get out of the plane and the rest couldn't.

While on the ground, Litcher told me, "When you tucked next to Richards' plane, you put us in line for the next stick."

We waited for transportation, which by the way, turned out to be a one-horse cart with a guard dog. Along the road somewhere, sirens were heard and an ambulance stopped at the wagon and offered to take me. My back was damaged, and I was in pain. But I knew they wouldn't do anything about it. I knew the hospital was full, and if I went along… That's the last I saw of Litcher and Thompson. Months later, an officer who was with Litcher and Thompson in the hospital saw me and told me that Litcher said, "If you ever see Hyde, tell him Thompson didn't make it. He lost too much blood." Thompson died that night.

I reached Frankfort, Germany, for interrogation at the Dulag camp. Sagan, Germany, was where Stalag III was. The captain of the interrogation became very angry with me because I said I didn't know anything. The interrogator reached down in a file and pulled out a green card. My name and my father's name were on it. The interrogator wanted to make sure each person was a true prisoner of war and not someone dropped behind the lines. The interrogator already knew the names of the crew that had been found.

Walter Krowal, of the 745th Squadron, said that when he got back to Italy after Blechhammer, people on the ground said, "The 746th Squadron suffered the greatest losses of any squadron on any mission before or after."

Years later I asked the Group Leader why he did what he did (changed course) and he said they'd lost an engine. I said, "I've lost engines before and I stayed in formation. You could have stayed in the lead." And I said, "Where was your white handkerchief?" Disabled planes wave a white handkerchief. He didn't answer me.

# EPILOGUE

After the war, Dad wasn't sure what he wanted to do. One of his younger brothers remembers driving around with him to look at small airfields. Dad thought about buying one or maybe flying small airplanes. Instead of doing that, he bought Barker Dry Goods store from his uncle, Reuben A. Smith. He had always been close to this aunt and uncle, and he had majored in Business Administration in college, before the war, so this made sense. It was a small, family-run store that his uncle had owned since the early 1920s. Douglas married Mina Hetherley in 1949, and they had two children, Beth and Paul. In the early 1950s, Douglas also bought this same uncle's insurance agency.

I think of our life in Barker, NY, a small village of 500 people then and now, as the Ozzie and Harriet time, growing up there in the 1950s and 60s. We had lots of fun with our extended families: picnics, swimming, skiing, and boating on Lake Ontario (two miles away), not to mention hunting and fishing with Dad. It was such a nice time for my brother and me to grow up in a safe, secure family. Dad hardly ever talked about the war. I do remember him singing "She Wore a Yellow Ribbon," and he did keep up with his bombardier, Dan Curran, over the years. We visited him and his family in St. Louis, and they came to Barker. In 1994, we visited Joseph Nickel, his nose turret gunner, in a nursing home in Rochester, NY.

In the mid 1970s, when Dad retired, he and Mom moved to Waxhaw, NC, to volunteer with JAARS (Jungle Aviation and Radio Service), which served around the world as a support organization for Wycliffe Bible Translators. It was in 1986 that he read in the *Charlotte Observer* that a 456th Bomb Group reunion would be held at Colorado Springs, CO. That was the first time he had heard about the 456th Bomb Group Association. He and Mom went that year and attended many, many other reunions after that. He opened up about the war after going to his first reunion, renewed friendships, found men alive who had been shot down, and started writing up the experiences covered in this book.

He would be so proud of his grandson, David, for taking the initiative to enhance his memoir with pictures and maps and for arranging to have it published.

— *Beth Richards Godfrey, daughter of Douglas Richards*

# ABOUT THE AUTHOR

DOUGLAS COULTER RICHARDS, or Doug to many, was born on January 30, 1918, on the family farm in Warren's Corners, New York, while World War I was still raging in Europe. He grew up on the dairy farm, lived through the Great Depression, and went to college at Syracuse University, graduating in 1940.

He had many hobbies, including golf, hunting, fishing, gardening, making furniture, reading, and traveling. He and his wife Mina traveled to many 456th Bomb Group reunions over the years.

After living his life to the fullest, Doug passed away on March 11, 2010, and is buried with his wife in Cambria, New York. He is survived by his two children, Beth and Paul, plus many grandchildren and great-grandchildren.

*Doug Richards going hunting with grandson David Godfrey, 1998.*

www.hellgatepress.com

Made in the USA
Middletown, DE
03 July 2023

34414482R00096